Soul Intuition

The Sacred Practice of Connecting to Your God Given Spiritual Gifts

Allison Larsen

Published by ChickLit

First Edition

Copyright © Allison H. Larsen 2016

All rights reserved. No part of this publication may be reproduced, stored in a retrieval system, or transmitted, in any form, or by any means, electronic, mechanical, photocopying, recording, or otherwise, without the prior consent of the publisher.

Sale of this book without a front cover may be unauthorized. If the book is coverless, it may have been reported to the publisher as "unsold or destroyed" and neither the author nor the publisher may have received payment for it.

http://www.soulintuition.com

ISBN: 978-1-935598-95-4

Printed in the United States of America

Table of Contents

Foreword vii
Introduction..x

THE SUCCESSFUL SOUL

Soul Intuition: Balancing Body and Spirit 23
Success and Happiness: The AND or WHEN Decision 33
Success for the Soul: Just for Today 45

BECOMING EMPOWERED

Empowering Change: Do What You Want and Be Successful... 59
Empowered to Shine: Becoming a Lighthouse 73
Empowered Through Giving: How Helping is Healing 83

EMBRACING LOVE

Loving All Layers: Healing from the Inside Out 95
A Loving Perception: Learning to See the Good 111
Vision of Love: Learning to See the Divine Within 127

SOUL INTUITION

Soul Action: The World's Way vs. God's Way 145
Soul Weakness: Finding Gifts 157
Soul Intuition Implemented... 171
References.. 189
Acknowledgments 191

About the Author 193

Your greatness is not defined by your accomplishments. You can accomplish great things because of who you are.

~Allison Larsen

Foreword

Congratulations, my friend. You are holding a treasure in your hands. As a member of the human family, you already possess the gifts, talents, inspiration and determination to be hugely successful, wildly happy, and passionately purposeful.

Do you believe that? Are you experiencing it?

If your answer to either of those questions is "No" or "Not fully" then this book is perfect for you. Far too many of us walk through life feeling incapable and inept, and far too many books try to teach us how to fix our broken selves. Soul Intuition is radically different. As you read, you will be introduced into a new thought paradigm. One where you are not fixing what is broken, but rather finding the courage to tap into what is Godly, dynamic, and powerful inside of you. If that sounds scary, don't worry. It is! Living a ridiculously happy life doesn't happen without skill. Fortunately for you, you have Allison Larsen to guide you through the process.

Years ago, a friend of mine told me, "I'm not like you, Amy. I am not naturally positive and happy all the time." I laughed, and at first she thought I was laughing at her! I quickly explained that I was laughing because her comment made me realize how much effort I put into being positive and happy almost all the time. You see, our human family has never lived in such a "loud" time. Our Western culture has become almost obsessed with busy schedules, social media, feeling overwhelmed and hyper-productivity. The result of our desire to be "plugged in" all the time is that we have lost something divine inside of ourselves. We have forgotten the ancient art of accessing our Soul Intuition.

I first met Allison Larsen when she became my client. But I fell in love with Allison when I became hers. As a business owner, I was overwhelmed with the demands of running a rapidly expanding business, and balancing my family. My full life demands that I be on top of my game. And yet, I was in a season of my life where I felt that connecting to inspiration was a daily struggle. I wanted it. I created time for it. But, something was still missing. During the course of working with Allison, I felt every piece click into place. The fear and worry I was experiencing moved on. The discipline I lacked, I found. The clarity I needed came into focus. And the most exciting part was that the progress came from inside me. I was able to stop looking for answers around me and start tapping into my God-given ability to receive clear and direct inspiration. I was living a highly connected life.

Let me ask, what could happen for you if you were living a highly connected life? What could happen for you if you were dialed in to your Soul Intuition?

Reading this book will take you on a journey into yourself. Some stops on the journey will look like bad neighborhoods where you would like to just keep driving and pretend you were never there. Stop anyway, look around, love yourself and forgive yourself for allowing that neighborhood to take root in your mind and heart. Other stops on the journey will be the most delightful, rewarding destinations and you will wonder why you had never been there before. I encourage you to fully engage as you read this book. Be open, be brave, and be present. Can a book really change your life? Probably not. But implementing the principles you read in a book? That can change more than just your life. It can change the world.

I am so grateful that Allison has taken this step to take her tools, her knowledge, her inspiration to the masses. Allison doesn't just talk about Soul Intuition, she lives it. She is a walking, breathing, beautiful example of how to live a highly connected life guided by Inspiration. She knows her talents and she uses them to bless lives daily.

This book is a must read and a necessary addition to your personal development library.

If you love this book as much as I know you will, will you do me a favor? Share the book. Share it with your family, your friends, your neighbors and your team members. In a world where darkness seems so prevalent, we have the ability to find our light and then spread it to others. I look forward to your journey of self-discovery. And I look forward to seeing a world filled with the goodness of Soul Intuition readers.

To your Success,

Amy Walker

Executive Business Coach/ Professional Speaker/ Radio Host and Author of *Walk Your Talk: Take Ownership and Lead Like You Mean It*

Introduction

Do you feel like there is something missing? If you have that empty feeling in the pit of stomach, your soul is hungry. Your spirit knows your potential and your body was designed to carry out that inherent mission. If you are not doing what you were designed to do, if you are not using the gifts you have been given to their greatest possible extent then your soul will let you know.

When we connect with our God-given gifts, a flame is lit within us. As we share that fire with those around us, we are helping them to light their wicks, spreading light wherever we go and making the world a warmer place. That fire feeds our soul.

You know what I am talking about. You have seen people who seem to glow with confidence and radiate goodness and truth. Those are the people who attract others, who attract success and who attract true happiness. You can be one of those people. You can magnify your light, dispelling shadows of self-doubt and creating abundance if your life and helping others do the same. It is a great way to live, full of purpose, fulfillment and true meaning. You will feel full, because you are living your life to the fullest.

That is Soul Intuition.

No one can discover your God-given gifts for you. You must learn to look within and do that for yourself. There are many self-help books, gurus, mentors and words of advice from well-meaning friends and family who love us. These are great resources when used as self-reflection tools. But, when we rely on others to tell us who we should be and what we should do, there is a problem. The blueprint lies within you and you are the architect of your life. You are the only one that truly knows how you are feeling. No one else has experienced being you. No one else has experienced the exact same life as you. You are the only one that determines if you are truly happy or not, no one can experience that for you. Ultimately, success looks different for everyone.

What would success look like for you?

It is important to have your end vision in mind. Where would you like to end up? I am not even necessarily talking about specifics, although they can be helpful. I am asking you what it is going to take for you to feel like you are making a difference in the world, like you are doing what you were meant to do. Are you settling for a job that just pays the bills, but that you are not passionate about? Are you settling for mediocre relationships that are shallow and not fulfilling? In what areas of your life are you compromising your happiness rather than making an impact?

My dear friend once told me that he admired me, that my life seemed great and that I made it look easy.

The truth is that my life is not easy, but I am determined and I work hard to create what I want in life. The key was learning where to focus my energy. I have discovered that greatness comes from within and radiates out. If I work on me, I will attract the things I want in life.

This book is about you. It is not about who to contact to find success or how to find a great business partner. This book is not about marketing or how to invest your capital to create great wealth. This book is about you becoming successful by investing in yourself and recognizing your wealth of hidden talents and gifts. It is about you learning to look within to find your answers, the ones that are unique to you and will help you find greater success and happiness.

Have you ever taken the time to sit down and make a list of your talents, to think about what unique gifts you have offer to the world?

We all have greatness within and God has given us everything we need to succeed, the key is to discover it, to connect with our soul, to recognize the potential within ourselves. Once we do that, we have the power to create whatever we want in our lives.

WE HAVE THE POWER TO CREATE THE LIFE WE WANT.

All we need to do is look within for the power and answers we need to succeed. That is Soul Intuition.

Many of my clients are looking for answers about the direction they are supposed to go with their lives. They want to know what to do or how to do what they do better. At first people are shocked when I tell them that I am not going to give them the answers to their questions. What I tell them is that I am going to guide them, teach them how to use their Soul Intuition so they can be empowered to find their own solutions.

Many people are waiting for someone to tell them how to be happy or successful. They want a step-by-step formula that works. Are you one of them? Be honest with yourself. I mean an ultimate solution would be awesome!

The problem is that the one equation doesn't work when you have different factors, and each of us have different experiences, gifts and passions that all factor into finding our own success. While someone is waiting to discover that non-existent, magic, one-size-fits-all formula, they are not pursuing their dreams or living the joyful life that they could be experiencing.

I often see people living far below their potential and far below their level of true happiness. Are you living up to your potential of happiness?

I have found true happiness as I have been able to use my God-given gifts to help myself and others become more self-aware and grow closer to their divine source of truth and light. I have found true happiness at the end of each day when I have been able to reflect back and know that I have used my unique talents to support someone who was prepared to listen and was in turn ready to support and help the people in their life. I have found true happiness as I have shared my message with others.

As I have mentored thousands of people around the world, I have learned that the most effective way for someone to find true happiness is for me to act as a mirror, a true reflection allowing them see who they are and what they are capable of. The answers discovered are as different as each person's physical reflection. And thank goodness we are all unique, that we each have an individual blueprint for making the world a better place. As great as he is, could you imagine what it would be like if there were a billion Tony Robbins on the planet?

What I have found is that although the talents, messages and personalities of my clients differ, there are some constants. They feel truly happy when they connect emotionally to the people in their lives. They feel truly happy when they engage in physically serving the world around them in a meaningful way. And, they feel truly happy when they experience the spiritual peace that comes from living their unique purpose. So where do we find out how to live up to our divine potential for true happiness, purpose and fulfillment?

There are two places we can look for answers, outside ourselves or within. Many look to the world to define them and tell them what to do. The danger of looking for solutions outside of ourselves is that we let others define us and determine our success and happiness. But there is no consistency in these outside sources, the world is constantly changing the definition of success. If we look within, however, we are empowered to define ourselves and create the life we want. In reality, all that needs to happen for any of us to accomplish greater happiness and fulfillment is to start looking within. We define ourselves, we define our success, we define our own happiness.

I have helped people from all walks of life find their greatness by teaching them to use their Soul Intuition, the art of looking inside themselves to discover their God-given gifts and divine potential. Are you ready to discover yours and begin living the life you were born to live? Are you going to stop settling and start creating the life you want?

As an intuition mentor, reiki master, foot zone practitioner and personal trainer, I have found that there is no one size fits all diet or success formula out there. What I have learned is that we came designed with a blueprint for success imprinted our soul. We must be willing to do the work, though. What good is a blueprint without a construction crew to manifest the design? Get your toolbox ready, my friends. I am about to give you all the tools you need to construct a successful life by tapping into your Soul Intuition.

The components of a soul are the body and spirit. Our body is designed to tell us what we need to find greater health and wellness on all levels, we just need to learn to recognize what it is telling us. The universe is set up for our success, we simply need to learn to ask our spirit where our place in it is. This is called intuition.

Intuitive living is really about connecting with your soul to discover your individual plan of happiness and success. Soul Intuition is the sacred practice of connecting with your God-given gifts to discover your individual plan for happiness and your unique blueprint for success. I use the word *sacred* because Soul Intuition is something I highly value and I know you will too as you come to recognize the great potential and importance of your life purpose. I use the word *practice*, because self-discovery is never-ending. Even once we have uncovered a gift, we can continue to discover its many uses, creating the life we want and bettering the world around us.

That doesn't mean there won't be trials or hardships. Learning to look within and following the blueprint that will lead to our ultimate success and fulfillment does not mean that there won't be a need for work and for struggle, for that is how dreams are built. With the intensification of happiness comes the magnification of sorrow. With extreme success comes the risk of complete failure. But, ask yourself, can one truly appreciate happiness and success if they have not experienced sadness and failure? Would we really appreciate the sweetness of life if we never knew bitter?

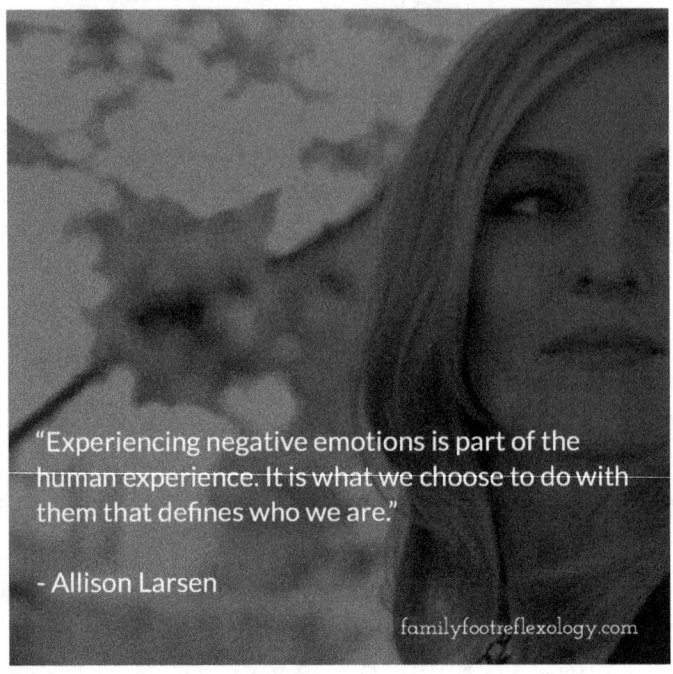

Something I have learned is that emotions come as a package deal. In order to feel great fulfillment and joy, you will most likely have moments of failure and pain. Experiencing negative emotions is part of the human experience. It is what we choose to do with them that defines who we are. If this is not something you are willing to accept, then read no further. If it is worth it to you to experience moments of pain and failure for a lifetime of fulfillment and joy, then this is the book for you. You will not become perfect, but you will be empowered to move towards success. Forward motion comes as you are willing to be honest with yourself about where you are on your journey in life and what you are experiencing.

We all know somebody who seems "perfect." EVERY Facebook post contains children who are always happy, profile pictures that seem like they were professionally shot, and a plethora of dream vacation photos. Their captions read something like,

"We are having a blast at the beach on our 6-month vacation!"
or
"My little Mary just did the sweetest thing and raised 2 million dollars for the local homeless shelter selling cookies!"

Okay, so maybe these are a exaggeration, but you get the idea. Some people appear to have amazing lives with no problems. They are always happy and positive. Negative emotions and problems seem foreign to them.

I used to get annoyed when I read those posts and was around perpetually positive individuals. Then, one day I realized I was one of them. I was always putting on a show. I wore a smile (along with my best outfit) every day come rain or shine. I threatened my children with everything but their lives if they weren't on their best behavior in public. I was afraid people may think I wasn't happy, and if I wasn't happy they may think my life wasn't perfect, and if they knew I wasn't perfect they might not like me. The problem was, despite appearances, I wasn't happy, I wasn't perfect and the people who thought I was resented me for it!

Luckily, I was blessed to have some amazing individuals placed in my path who helped me realize this one important truth, **negative emotions are part of the human experience**.

All of us experience negative feelings and all of us have problems. Hurt, pain, disappointment, discouragement and hopelessness are real and there is no reward for pretending they don't exist. In fact, research has shown that people who are perfectionists often suffer from severe anxiety.

So, what is the answer? How do we find real positivity in a world full of negative emotions and experiences? We discover how to tap into our Soul Intuition so we can learn from the hard times, discover our God-given gifts and look within to fulfill our divine potential. The negative emotions wont go away, but we can learn how to process them and even use them to our advantage.

People who learn to learn get to grow, and growth is positive. Let me repeat that, people who learn to learn, get to grow. Learning and growing is about being transparent and raw. It is admitting that you experienced something less than perfect, allowing yourself to feel the pain and then using that experience to grow into something greater.

A meaningful human experience is about owning your negative feelings and life-trials and then sharing what you learned so we can all help each other out during this crazy ride we call life. It's about making your mess your message by giving others around you the opportunity to learn from your counsel rather than consequence. So, let's get real and raw. Let's learn to learn so we can grow and help others around us grow as well. And, for goodness sakes, let's help each other out by being more honest with ourselves and others, by embracing the positive along with the negative and admitting that we are all human.

You will learn more about me and my story in subsequent chapters, but I feel like I need to tell you something from the get go so that there are no false expectations or disappointments. I have times in my life when I feel helpless, hopeless and worthless. I am not perfect. I am not a millionaire. I am not famous. If perfection, money and fame are your only goals then this book is not for you.

Over the past decade I have experienced great joy and fulfillment. I have a peace that comes from having discovered my talents and God-given gifts and using them to help others. I have a wealth of knowledge and tools that I have used to create the life I want. I know how to help people find joy, fulfillment and peace. I have come to learn that any success experienced in life without these three things is empty and shallow. So, if you want a deep, true, meaningful life then you will find the tools you need to create what you want within these chapters. You will discover your God-given gifts through the sacred practice of Soul Intuition.

Part 1
THE SUCCESSFUL SOUL

When we are able to release feelings of fear from our being, a space is created for us to discover the success within our soul that has been lying dormant for years, waiting to emerge.

~Allison Larsen

Once the soul awakens, the search begins and you can never go back. From then on, you are inflamed with a special longing that will never again let you linger in the lowlands of complacency and partial fulfillment. The eternal makes you urgent. You are loath to let compromise or the threat of danger hold you back from striving toward the summit of fulfillment.

~ John O'Donohue, Anam Cara: A Book of Celtic Wisdom

1

Soul Intuition: Balancing Body and Spirit

Dedicated to my parents, who first taught me to look within.

What is the soul?
The soul consists of our body and our spirit, the physical and the metaphysical put together. In order to care for our soul, to allow it to thrive, we must honor both aspects. We have a body that needs food, exercise and rest. We have emotions, stress and pain that we experience. In many ways our body is limited, sometimes by physical illnesses or age. We experience emotions like fear or frustration that can become roadblocks stopping us in our tracks.

Then, there is our spirit. Our spirit knows no boundaries. It knows what our capabilities are and wants to grow at a rate that often exceeds our physical limitations. In a sense, our spirit is limitless but it must honor the body. It is like wanting to run a marathon without training. No matter how willing your spirit, if you body has not gone through proper conditioning, you will not be ready.

Have you ever had moments in your life where you wanted to run faster than you had strength? Have you had those times when you have wanted to accomplish more than you were physically able, when you had more ideas and ambitions than you had the time or strength to complete? Maybe you tried and your body rebelled and gave in to fatigue or you got sick after "running yourself ragged." Our bodies are frustrating, yet amazing that way. They let us know when they need attention and care.

The opposite can also be true. Sometimes our body is able and willing to go, but our spirit is down and feels unmotivated or even broken. Maybe you are healthy, but feel stuck in life. Maybe you have a sense that there is more you could be doing, that there is some greater purpose or mission that you are not fulfilling.

Sound familiar?

The truth is that we cannot live up to our divine potential without our body and we cannot complete our mission here on earth without our spirit. Yet, our body and our spirit don't always co-exist in harmony. Sometimes they are fighting against one another. The solution is to find balance, a way to allow both to thrive and compliment one another. When the body and spirit work together in harmony, the soul will flourish, creating an environment that will allow you to use your God-given gifts and talents to fulfill your divine potential.

> When the body and spirit can work together in harmony, the soul will flourish, creating an environment that will allow you to use your God-given gifts and talents to fulfill your divine potential.
>
> soulintuition.com

Quiz

Take this quiz to help discover the current level of harmony within your soul. Answer each question on a scale of 1-5, with 1 being never and 5 being always.

1. You have plenty of energy to complete all of your tasks each day.
2. You feel that you are carrying out your purpose here on earth.
3. At the end of the day you have a sense of fulfillment.
4. You are generally happy.
5. You take care of your body and consider yourself to be healthy.

If your score is below 20, your soul needs help to blossom. If your score was below 10 I suggest immediate intervention. Your soul is in critical condition!

What should you do if you identify that you need help? Begin by applying the principles you will learn in this book. You will find a greater balance and inner peace. Your body and your spirit will begin to work more harmoniously to manifest the life you were meant to live.

What is intuition?

Intuition is the ability to connect with our soul, to listen and find answers from within. In order to find those answers, we must learn to be still enough to hear what our spirit is trying to tell us and we must be aware of our physical needs so that we can honor the signals our body is sending. This involves focus and finesse. It requires peace and connection to our divine source of truth and light. It requires letting go of the negative emotions that are pulling us down and replacing them with positive emotions that help buoy us and strengthen us.

My clients who have learned to live intuitively know where to find the answers. They know their destination in life and although they don't know what speed bumps or surprises they may experience along the way, they are confident that those stumbling blocks can become stepping stones leading to success as they honor their intuition and are open to learning from their mistakes and misfortunes. They understand that trials only help us grow and that our mess often becomes our most powerful message.

Have you ever wondered what your life mission and purpose is? Have you ever questioned why you were experiencing a certain trial or hardship? Have you ever felt that there was more to life? The answers to all these questions and many more are there, inside of you. You just need to listen.

Quiz

Take this quiz to determine your current ability to listen to your intuition. Answer each question or a scale of 1-5 with 1 being never and 5 being always.

1. You participate in regular meditation or self-reflection.
2. You are able to easily express your feelings through writing or some other healthy outlet.
3. You are confident in your ability to make decisions.
4. You feel peaceful most of the time.
5. You have a clear vision of what you want in life.

If your score is below 20, then you are not currently experiencing the benefits of intuitive living. If you scored low, don't worry, there is hope! The good news is that your blueprint for success and happiness is in there. No one can take that away and it will never be lost. All you need to do is learn how to find it.

> "There are two places we can look for answers, outside ourselves or within. The danger of looking for solutions from without is that we allow others to define us. When we look within we are empowered to define ourselves and create the life we want.
>
> All that needs to happen for us to accomplish greater happiness and fulfillment is to start looking within, to tap into our soul intuition, the art of looking within to discover individual God-given gifts and divine potential."
> Allison Larsen
>
> soulintuition.com
> allisonlarsen.com

As you read the remainder of this book and implement the action steps given at the end of each chapter, you will learn how to live intuitively. Remember to be patient with yourself. It is okay if you go slow, taking time between chapters to do the steps. I also give you permission to read the book as often as you need. Just make sure you implement at least one new tool each time.

I saw an anonymous quote the other day that said, "If you are persistent you will get it. If you are consistent, you will keep it." Be persistent in your implementation of the tools you are about to learn and then do them consistently. If you do this, your life will change. You will be able to use your Soul Intuition to discover your God-given gifts and fulfill your divine potential.

What is Soul Intuition?

Soul Intuition is born when the body and spirit are balanced, co-existing in harmony and the owner is taking the time and steps necessary to look for answers from within. When you use Soul Intuition, you have the ability to recognize and use your God-given gifts and talents so you can fulfill your divine potential. After reading the definitions above and taking the quizzes, you now have a greater awareness of your current level of Soul Intuition.

So, how can you heighten your ability to access this powerful practice, the art of looking within to connect to your God-given gifts? The answer is simple, you must let go of the things in life that are preventing you from living to your fullest potential. My experience working with thousands of people over the past decade has helped me identify the three most common destructive and negative emotions preventing people from recognizing their God-given gifts and living to their fullest potential.

Fear.
Helplessness.
Inadequacy.

In the following chapters you will learn the tools needed to let go of the negative emotions preventing you from using your Soul Intuition. You will learn to replace them with powerfully positive emotions that build and lift your soul.

Success.
Empowerment.
Love.

Once you learn to let go of fear, helplessness and inadequacy you will be ready to invite success, empowerment and love into your life. You will be ready for soul intuition. You will be able to recognize your God-given gifts. You will be able to live the life you were designed to live.

Are you ready to begin? Are you ready to use your talents to help yourself and to make the world around you a better place?

I believe in you. You may be wondering how I can say that. After all I don't even know you. But, what I do know through my personal and professional experiences of working with thousands of people from all over the world and from all walks of life is that when someone learns to use their Soul Intuition to access their divine blueprint, they will find success, empowerment and the ability to love themselves. After all, this is your success plan, not mine. There is no way that something that was designed just for you and tailored to your individual gifts, talents and experiences can fail you.

That is the beauty of Soul Intuition. You do not have to wonder if you will succeed or fail. You do not need to question whether or not this program will work for you or if this book will help you. It will. All you need to do is believe in yourself enough and have the faith to act on the steps you will be given. Take time to write down your thoughts and feelings as you read each chapter. Every time that you get an "ah ha" moment or have a breakthrough, make sure to write it down.

I believe that there are no coincidences. If this book is in your hands right now, it means that you are ready. You are prepared for what you are about to learn. Perhaps you have struggled to find your place in the universe and your purpose in life that you prayed for something to help you discover your unique niche. This book could be that answer. Maybe you already feel like you have discovered your divine mission, but want to know how to make the best use of your God-given gifts. This book will help you learn how to implement your unique talents to the fullest. Or, there may be those of you who are struggling with getting your body on board with what your spirit wants to do or vice versa. That can be a very frustrating thing to feel like you are fighting yourself all the time. This book will teach you how to let go of your frustration and make space for harmony.

What is the reason this book is in your life right now? Why is now the time for you to learn these life-changing skills? If you are ready for change and committed to bettering your life then keep reading. You will learn how to be successful now.

You must live in the present, launch yourself on every wave, find your eternity in each moment. Fools stand on their island of opportunities and look towards another land. There is no other land, but this.

~ Henry David Thoreau

2

Success and Happiness: The AND or WHEN Decision

Dedicated to Tammy, my beautiful friend and mentor.

How many times have you said, "I'll be happy when I lose weight, finish school, get that raise…"

The list goes on and on.

The problem with this mentality is that we aren't finding success in the moment. Each minute that we haven't achieved our goal, reason would say we are not happy. I don't know about you, but I would rather be happy more often than not. I would rather find happiness now, not next week, next month or next decade!

"The most important thing is to enjoy your life-to be happy-it's all that matters."
~Audrey Hepburn

If we are constantly setting ourselves up for failure, we get comfortable with failing. We become victims of self-sabotage. Whether we like it our not, our brain subconsciously leads us to decisions that feel comfortable and familiar.

On the other hand, if we are used to feeling successful then we will recognize opportunities for success in our lives. I see it all the time. People who take the time to celebrate their achievements and find joy in the journey of life are more likely to accomplish their goals.

Years ago I managed a gym. Each January a huge crowd of people would flock to my facility with new resolutions for weight loss and better health. The numbers would skyrocket. These newcomers seemed committed and determined to make changes in their lives. But by March about half of them quit showing up and the numbers would continue to decline over the next few months. I watched many "determined" people drop like flies, each one giving up on their goals and, essentially, on themselves.

This always intrigued me. Why were people who seemed so committed and determined failing? And what was the difference between the many who abandoned their resolutions and the few that stuck with it? I began to pay attention and started to notice a pattern between those that accomplished their goals and those that did not.

The successful clients always said that they were happy AND they would like to take better care of their bodies. They would do exercises they enjoyed. They were smiling. They were realistic with the amount of time they spent in the gym, recognizing that although fitness is important, it is not the only thing in life. They exercised AND found happiness all around them in the now. They took time to celebrate their successes, often ending each visit to the gym with a big smile and a comment about what they had accomplished that day.

The less successful group, the ones that appeared in January and disappeared soon after would inevitably show up the next year a few pounds heavier and even more determined to get fit. People in this group would often say that they would be happy WHEN they lost weight. Generally they had an all or nothing mentality. I would often hear unrealistic goals and expectations.

"I am going to come to the gym everyday for three hours, seven days a week."
"I am going to lose 20 lbs in the next 10 days."
"I am going to fit into a dress 5 sizes smaller by my sister's wedding next month."

Okay, so maybe these are a slight exaggeration, but only slight. Clients in this group that missed a day, had a bad weigh-in or didn't drop a dress size in a week, were finished. Game over. They were critical of themselves and I often heard a curse word or two escape when they failed to meet their unrealistic performance goals.

Have you ever set a long-term goal or made a resolution that you did not achieve despite your best intentions? Why?

Our souls are designed to seek those things that bring us happiness. Our spirits seek compliments and validation. Our bodies seek pleasure and results. We are built to succeed and we need constant reminders that we are successful now.

A person's soul gets needy if they are always focusing on the future, the WHEN. Just like a seed, a soul needs constant, even daily nourishment to thrive. Every day you need to sprinkle it with compliments and put it in a sunny place where it can feel all warm and good. By doing this each day your soul can thrive, and a soul that thrives feels peaceful, purposeful AND happy. A soul that thrives connects with their God-given gifts and produces the fruit of transcendence, the ability to use those talents to better the world around them.

We can't just plant a seed, ignore it and say that WHEN it produces fruit we will nourish it, WHEN I feel happy, then I will take care of myself. Plants will not flourish that way, and neither will your soul.

"A provocative new research article from Oxford University...(found) that happy, successful people who make positive life choices all showed greater connectivity in brain regions associated with high-level cognition.
The researchers found that people who scored higher in positive measures of lifestyle and behavior had stronger functional connectivity between brain regions associated with memory, language, imagination and theory of mind (the ability to attribute mental states to oneself and others)." (Gregoire, 2015)

People who choose to look for the good in the present, who choose to find joy in the journey, are the ones who are thriving. They are not only happier in general but might even be smarter.

We, each one of us, are meant to experience joy in this life. The universe is set up to give us that joy every day. We just have to remember to look for it. All the answers for what we need to feel happy and fulfilled now are there inside of us. All we need to do is use our Soul Intuition to uncover them.

I am not saying that goals are bad. I am not saying that we should be content with whatever we are handed in life and not strive to make it better. What I am saying is that if we forget to find happiness now, our lives will be a shadow of what they could have been. I see people all the time that are so focused on future goals that they practically trip over the many blessings placed at their feet.

Throughout the years, I have seen clients from many backgrounds but the problems they experience are not so different. What differentiates my clients from each other in the beginning is how they have decided to handle those problems.

Anne came to me 3 years ago. She had recently been diagnosed with terminal cancer and was hoping to find some peace as she neared the end of her life. Anne was the mother of 9 children ranging in ages from 8-23. She had a loving, supportive husband and extended family. Each time she came to see me she was smiling and I would often hear her say, "I am not going to let this thing beat me." At first I thought she was talking about the cancer, that she wasn't going to let it kill her. But what I came to realize is that she was talking about her mental, emotional and spiritual state of being and not her physical death. She was not going to let the disease defeat her ability to live her life, dampen her dreams or halt her hope. She had cancer AND she was happy. She had cancer AND she was still living the life she wanted.

She did not let it "beat her." Anne would crack jokes each time I saw her and tell me about her children's events with that proud mother gleam in her eye. Before we parted after each session she would always ask if there was anything she could do for me! As I got to know a few of her children, I also came to know that they felt loved and supported by their mother even during the height of her battle with cancer.

The last time I saw Anne she was in the hospital, barely able to move. Upon seeing me, she offered her best smile and through ragged breaths said, "I am not going to let this beat me!" She had cancer AND she chose not to let it beat her.

At her funeral Anne was remembered as a wonderful mother, dear friend and faithful daughter who remained true to herself until the end of her life. Her powerful legacy lives on in the hearts of all those who knew her.

Like Anne, Susan was another client who had been diagnosed with cancer. Her cancer was not terminal but, unlike Anne, she was allowing her illness to define her. Even on her first call to schedule an appointment, she introduced herself as "Susan, a cancer patient." True, she was a patient and she had cancer, but what a sad title to follow your name. Why not, "Susan, a mother, lawyer, and passionate person, who happens to be fighting cancer." See the difference?

Susan felt hopeless and defeated. She told me repeatedly that she would be happy WHEN her cancer was gone and that she could resume life WHEN she was cured. The first two times I saw her, she spent over half of our session telling me about the things she could not do, how horrible the medication was and how disappointed she was about how her life was going.

Fortunately, I was able to work with Susan and help her shift her mental attitude. She began to see that her life was not over, nor did she have to put it on hold waiting for the cancer to be gone. Susan began replacing WHEN with AND. Instead of telling herself and others that she had cancer and would be happy WHEN it was gone, she began saying that she had cancer AND was choosing to find happiness now.

"Folks are usually about as happy as they make their minds up to be."
~Abraham Lincoln

Fortunately, many of us are not struggling with a life threatening disease, but I do see many people who allow money, or the lack thereof, to be a major obstacle between them and happiness. Have you ever told yourself that you would be happy WHEN you could afford that new house or WHEN you had enough money to travel, or fill in the blank.

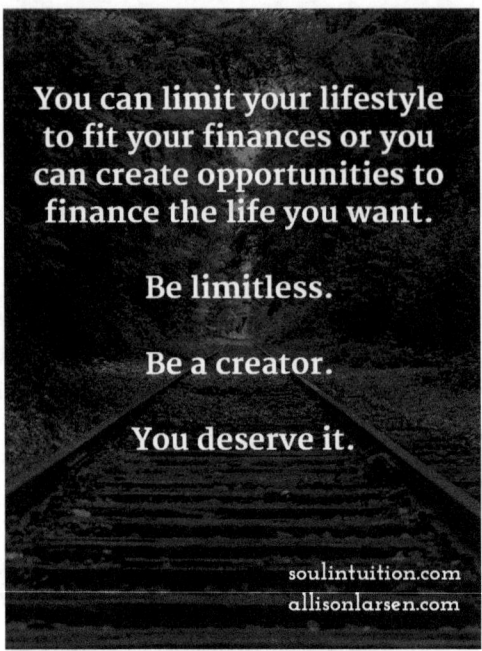

Why not decide to be happy now? Why not decide to be happy AND have that dream car on your vision board? Why not decide to be happy AND save up for that new house? People who report feeling happy, regardless of their bank balance or vacation destinations, are more successful in life.

WHEN is a limiting word. Whatever phrase precedes the word when is limited by the phrase that follows. For example, if someone says they will be happy WHEN they make more money, their level of happiness is directly determined by their level of income. When someone says they will be successful WHEN they get that new job, they are basing their level of success on someone else's decision to hire them or not.

AND is a creative word. We can create a phrase independent of any variables. For example, I can be happy AND have a certain level of income. My happiness does not depend on the money I make. I can be HAPPY and not get that job. I don't want my happiness to be determined by someone else.

"It isn't what you have or who you are or where you are or what you are doing that makes you happy or unhappy. It is what you think about it."
~Dale Carnegie

Do you want to live a life dependent on variables that are out of your control, or do you what to take charge of your life?

If you are living a life full of WHENs, you are living a limited life and missing out on the full happiness potential the universe has created for you. If you look to outside factors and people to determine your level of success, you will never reach it. If you want to change how you are feeling, then you have to be willing to change how you are thinking, create a new reality for yourself, create the life you want.

Take charge.

It really is your choice. You can decide if you want to put off the things you want in life or if you want to create the life you want now. How will you look back on your life at the end of the day? Will it have been a life full of joy AND happiness or life full of WHENs?

What are you waiting for? Take that leap, make the decision to be happy. I have never heard anyone that regretted feeling happy or complained that they had too much joy in their life. It takes work, but it is not hard. You can find happiness now.

It will take some effort and consistency to shift your mental thought pattern, but before you know it you will have created new habits in your life that will allow you to enjoy each day and find success, too.

It is so worth it!

If you are ready to change, to live a more successful life, there are a few simple action steps that you can take to start creating a new pattern. Get into a habit of doing these things daily and you will find success and happiness now!

"Happiness is when what you think, what you say, and what you do are in harmony."
~Mahatma Gandhi

ACTION STEPS

1. At the end of each day, journal about something you did that day that brought you happiness.
2. Set daily goals that will bring you happiness.
3. If you catch yourself saying that you will be happy WHEN (even if it is only in your mind), stop and replace the word WHEN with AND.

For example, replace "I will be happy WHEN I get that new car" to "I am happy AND I have a goal to get a new car."

Tomorrow is tomorrow. Future cares have future cures, and we must mind today.

~Sophocles

3

SUCCESS FOR THE SOUL: JUST FOR TODAY

Dedicated to Amy, who inspired me to begin.

Have you ever used the words *never* or the word *always* when making a commitment to your soul?

"I am always going to exercise."
"I will never yell at my kids."
"I will always stay calm and collected."
"I will never eat sugar again."

I am here to tell you, my friends, *always* and *never* are HUGE commitments to fulfill and easy promises to break. Now, I am not saying that you can't go your whole life without *never* doing something or that *always* is out of reach. But I would like you to consider a simple solution, a finite way to make easy and obtainable that which may seem daunting and out of reach. There is one phrase that will change your life: *just for today*.

"Just for today, I will take care of my body and exercise."

"Just for today, I will speak kindly to my children."
"Just for today, I will remain calm and focused."
"Just for today, I will fuel my body with healthy food."

Doesn't that sound better? If you aren't convinced, you may even want to try a little experiment. Try saying an *always* or *never* phrase out loud and then just take a moment to close your eyes and pay attention to how it sets with your soul. Do you feel pressure? Do you feel overwhelmed?

Now, try saying one of the "just for today" phrases. How does that feel? Does your soul give a sigh of relief? Does the goal seem obtainable? I bet you feel like you can accomplish that goal, that is realistic and within reach. After all, anyone can do something for just one day. Anyone can experience short-term success.

I have seen many new clients embrace an always or never mentality, an all or nothing approach. This philosophy causes them to wrestle with guilt, pain and failure. I admit, I tried this all or nothing mentality several times earlier in life as a motivation to stay in shape and reach my fitness goals. I was hard on myself. I felt like I failed more than I succeeded because I could never celebrate success. At the end of the day, I could not look in the mirror and feel that I had accomplished my goal. Even if I had been successful that day in my goal, I could not claim to be an overall success because I had not reached the final destination of never or always. I was constantly thinking about the next day or the next week, month or year and how in the world I was going to resist all the temptations, all the opportunities for failure. I felt overwhelmed and was less than excited about the future. All I could focus on was what I couldn't have or couldn't do, what I was denying myself for the rest of my life. I would eventually lose hope and motivation. I would give up. My soul was craving and yearning for daily compliments and I wanted so badly to feel successful, but that success seemed so far away and unattainable. Can you relate?

As humans, we tend to go into a flight or fight response whenever we feel overwhelmed and pressured. We are afraid. Our souls fear defeat and subconsciously we know that *always* and *never* are words that are setting us up for failure. We don't want to fail. Failure is painful, it affects our self esteem and our ability to commit to goals in the future.

Some people get so overwhelmed they give up on their goals completely, others become cynical after repeated failures and fight the idea of ever creating new goals. No matter which way you respond, the result is the same. You get sick of not feeling successful and your soul rebels against inadequacy.

As long as you use *always* and *never* in the wording of your goals, you are setting yourself up for failure. Simply replace them with the phrase, *just for today*, and your soul will be set up for success.

For a large portion of my life I embraced the *always* or *never* mentality, but in my early thirties, I found myself feeling discontent and unsuccessful in many areas of my life. I was constantly beating myself up for not accomplishing my unrealistic goals and it was affecting my self-esteem and my drive and desire to improve and move forward with more goals that I was only going to fail to achieve.

It was at this time that I was introduced to energy work. I was intrigued with the idea that energy was flowing through us and all around us, and that we could learn how to use that energy for good. I had always been able to sense things—certain feelings or energy surrounding a person, situation or environment. For a long time I thought this was a bad thing, something that made me odd. But, as I studied more about energy and the practice of reiki, I learned that it was a gift.

Rei refers to the Universal or God's light, love and energy that is all around us. *Ki* is the individual energy, or spirit that is in us.

Learning reiki has allowed me to act as a conduit between divine light, love and energy and the person's spirit on whom I am giving the reiki. That divine light, love and energy is healing for the soul, creating a loving environment that allows for homeostasis on the physical, mental, emotional and spiritual levels.

In order to act as a conduit, the person performing the reiki needs to be still and let go of the things that are causing tension in their life. There were many principles taught while learning reiki that allowed me to be at peace so that I could act as that conduit, including the principle I am teaching to you in this chapter.

When I was first introduced to the Just for Today Principle during reiki training, my soul literally gave a sigh of relief. This felt right to me. So, I tried it out. Each day I would start my goals with *just for today...* I found that at the end of almost every day I could celebrate success. And if I didn't, that was okay because there was another chance for success tomorrow. I was succeeding more than I was failing. Instead of beating myself up I felt good about the things I was accomplishing on a daily basis. I felt motivated and inspired to move forward in setting goals that would help me to create the life I wanted. Instead of thinking about how hard it was going to be to keep a commitment forever, I was just focusing on the one day. I can do anything for a day and so can you!

As I have embraced this mentality, I have also introduced this powerful Just for Today Principle to many of my clients and students and watched them succeed in areas of their lives that had been holding them back. Because they have experienced failure so many times with the *always* and *never* approach they had given up trying to do certain things because their souls did not want to experience those feelings of inadequacy and disappointment that accompanied the feeling of failure.

I have been blessed to work with Amy Walker, a very influential and globally renowned business coach who is a published author and speaker. She is very successful in many areas of her life but there was one obstacle, one road block that had been holding her back for years, until she was introduced to the Just for Today Principle. She had tried over and over again to master this particular area of her life, but had experienced many failures with her all or nothing approach. Now, she is able to embrace success almost every day and has turned her roadblock into a stepping stone leading to success. Recently, she shared the following on Facebook:

"Sometimes we struggle to commit long-term. We want to, we think we are there, but when it comes time to show up for our business, we hide. What if you shortened the commitment to today? And what if you lessened the commitment from changing everything all at once, to making a few critical adjustments? I guarantee your results would increase. I've been using these principles in my business for years. I've learned to be disciplined. I've learned to finish what I start, and I've learned to treat my time like it is gold! I use my time extremely well. BUT... I had a weakness. My weakness was food. I would commit to eating clean, then fall of the wagon after a few days. Once I was off, I tended to just binge on sugar and processed foods. Then I would feel guilty, beat myself up and get back on the wagon again. Only to repeat the cycle. An awesome mentor Allison Hildebrandt Larsen gave me the magic words to help me overcome my commitment cycle with food. 'Just for today...' Every day I start off my day with a commitment of 'Just for today...' This is my commitment this morning, 'Just for today I will honor myself and my body by eating clean. I will show up as my best self and pour my heart into all that I do. I will give my business my best, and I will give my family my best. I will stay free of stress and celebrate with joy and gratitude in my heart.' The power in this statement comes because it is 'Just for today...' I am human! I can't commit to that for the rest of my life. But I can do it for today. When moments of weakness come, I say those words, 'Just for today,' and I find strength in them. What amazing things can you commit to 'Just for today?'"

As Amy embraced the Just for Today Principle, she was able to change her way of thinking, setting her soul up for success everyday! She was able to overcome a major obstacle that she had been struggling with for years simply by changing a few simple words. How empowering.

The amazing thing is that as I watch clients like Amy get rid of personal roadblocks, they find success in other areas of their lives. Once our soul feels prosperous in one area, prosperity follows in many others because we are training our brains to let go of fear and embrace success. We are empowering ourselves to progress forward in life. We are teaching ourselves that we are capable of achieving the things we put our minds to.

What are your roadblocks? What areas have you attempted to master before and failed? If you are ready to feel prosperous and be successful, use the Just for Today Principle to approach your goals and see what a difference it makes in your life.

Why does this work? Why is it that when we break a goal down into a more finite time frame that we are more likely to find success?

The human brain is an amazing thing but somewhat limited in its ability to comprehend infinite amounts of time or space. For example, have you ever thought about eternity, a never-ending amount of time? Sure it may exist, but in our mortal form where everything has a beginning and an end, it is rather hard to contemplate and understand something that is never ending. And, what our brain doesn't understand, it can't figure out how to manifest.

Now you may be thinking that you want long-term goals and success. How can focusing on just today help us years down the road? Many of us are conditioned to think about the future and where we want to be in 5 or even 10 years down the road. Is this bad? Absolutely not! However, it is a long time away.

Use the Just for Today Principle consistently and you will create new habits and behaviors that will build on each other and help you reach your goals. One of my favorite verses from the Bible is Isaiah 28:10, in it the prophet gives us permission to work little by little towards our big goal,

"For precept must be upon precept, precept upon precept; line upon line, line upon line, here a little, and there a little."

When using the Just for Today Principle, you can be wise and pick goals that will lead you towards what you want in the future. Days will add up to weeks, weeks to months, and months to years. As you accomplish your daily goals you will find that they become automatic, you no longer have to think about them because they become habits. Once this happens, you can set new Just for Today goals that will lead you away from fear and closer to your ultimate vision of success.

Now that you know what to do, let's talk about why this technique works so well. I truly believe that knowledge brings power. Understanding how our souls (our body and spirit) work, liberates us from the fear of failure and empowers us to change.

Neuroscience studies have shown that using *never* to articulate a goal is particularly problematic because the subconscience mind does not hear negatives. For example lets take the phrase, "I will never eat sugar again." Our subconscience brain will focus on are the words eat, sugar and again. If I were to say to you, "do not scratch your nose," suddenly you are not only aware of your nose, you might even notice a little itch starting to form. That is not very effective!

Our minds will focus on the very things we are trying not to do. If there is something you want to avoid or stop doing, you should not state it in the phrasing of your goals. Focus on what you want to create and manifest in your life, not what you are trying to avoid doing. Instead of "I will never eat sugar," Amy found success in stating her goal as "Just for today, I will eat clean."

This is a very important step when using the "just for today" technique. Notice how all of the "just for today" statements listed above are worded in such a way to bring out the positive. Instead of saying, "Just for today, I will not yell at my children," I use the phrase, "Just for today, I will speak kindly to my children."

Where our thoughts go, our energy flows. If we are focusing on a negative thought, even if the intention of that focus is to not do it, we are still giving energy to something that we don't want to manifest in our life. Reframing your thoughts to focus only on the positive will enable you to put all your energy into what you want to create in your life, rather than what you do not want to manifest. Strive for a life full of success not failure.

Quit phrasing your goals in a manner that sets up your soul to fail. You deserve a prosperous and abundant life. Your soul wants you to be gentle and realistic. Simplify your life and break down your goals into a reasonable time frame. You can go to bed every night feeling like a success and if you don't, pick yourself up, dust off and remember there is always tomorrow.

As you begin to live the Just for Today Principle you will notice some big shifts within your soul. You will find that you beat yourself up less and compliment yourself more. Your will be able to let go of the fear of failure. You will begin to notice more of your divine qualities and your God-given gifts. You will experience a feeling of success on a day-to-day basis that will fuel you to create abundance in your life. You will also notice that each day brings you closer to the long-term goals that may have seemed out of reach in the past. It is a wonderful way to live and your soul will thank you.

I am going to give you a very simple formula that you can use with your goals and the "just for today" principle to set your soul up for success. Take the time to do these Action Steps if you want to create an environment conducive for personal growth. Above all, don't feel like you have to commit to this forever! Do it just for today. You will be able to let go of feelings of inadequacy as you set yourself up for regular success.

Just for today find happiness, success and peace. You deserve it!

ACTION STEPS

1. Make a list of goals you wanted to achieve in the past, but have not succeeded. These could be big things, such as getting out of debt, or small things, such as eating less sugar.
2. State the goal in a positive way, focusing on what you want to manifest in your life and using the *just for today* phrase. For example, "Just for today I will spend less than I make," or "Just for today, I will eat healthy food."
3. Select 5 (or fewer) daily goals to work on at a time. Keep your list in a place where you can review them daily.
4. Each morning state out loud your *just for today* goals while looking in the mirror.
5. Repeat tomorrow.

Part 2
Becoming Empowered

Souls who learn to silence the victim within will become victors over their own lives.

~Allison Larsen

Success is getting what you want.

~Dale Carnegie

4

EMPOWERING CHANGE: DO WHAT YOU WANT AND BE SUCCESSFUL

Dedicated to Bethany, who lights up the room with her smile.

I am here to tell you that you have to do nothing to be successful. Did you read that sentence again thinking there may have been a typo?

There is no mistake.

I have learned that to be really successful in life there is nothing you *have* to do, rather you must *want* to do the things that will lead you to success. It is very empowering. Let me explain.

How do you feel when someone tells you that you *have* to do something? It is no fun. If you are like me, you may resist, get a bit defiant and think, "I don't *have* to do anything!" And, that is true. You don't *have* to do much of anything in life.

The fact of the matter is that we do things because we want to. Sometimes we tell ourselves that there are things that we *have* to do, but the reality is that 99% of the time no one is forcing us to do anything. Almost every human action is voluntary, a choice we make. We decide each moment what we are going to do and we do it because we want to on either a conscious or subconscious level. If we view our actions and the choices we make as a decision, something we *want* to do rather than something we *have* to do, we will feel more empowered and in control of our lives, plus we will be more willing to do it. Here is an example.

When your car is running on empty, most people think, "I have to get gas."

That is not true.

You do not *have* to get gas. No one is holding a gun to your head and telling you that you have to drive to the gas station and fill your tank or else.

But, you probably *want* to get gas so you don't run out and become stranded on the side of the road. That would be really inconvenient and definitely more time consuming than driving to the nearest gas station to fill your tank. The alternative to taking the time to get fuel is worse, so you make a decision. You choose to take the time and effort required to get gas. You *want* to get gas so you don't have to face the consequences of running out. In this scenario, if you simply rephrase your self talk to replace the word *have* with the word *want*, you will find that you feel happy to go get gas, or at least not uber annoyed. You won't see it as much of a burden that you are forced to do, but as a good option that you have chosen.

Lets look at another common example.

How many times have you woken up in the morning, hit the alarm clock and your first thought was, "Ugh, I *have* to go to work today." You may feel grumpy and definitely do not jump out of bed with a shout of enthusiasm. You may drag your feet as you get ready and sulk out the door for another day of work, because it is something you *have* to do. It is just the daily grind.

In reality, you do not *have* to go to work at all. But, you probably *want* to. If you don't go to work you won't get paid. If you don't get paid then you won't be able to live in that beautiful house or drive that nice car or afford to feed your kids. You are choosing to go work because the benefits outweigh the cost. You *want* to go to work.

And, if work is really that miserable, maybe you *want* to change jobs.

It is when the costs or the price we pay outweighs the benefits that we should start asking ourselves if what we are choosing to do is really what we *want* to do. If we are doing something that we hate that is costing us peace of mind, happiness and healthy relationships but are seeing very few benefits, then we need ask ourselves if it is time for a change. As long as we are stuck in the mentality of feeling like we *have* to do something, as though there is no choice, then we feel helpless to make a change.

You are not helpless. Embrace your power by changing your thinking. Let go of the feeling that you *have* to do certain things and begin choosing to do *what* you want.

You can create whatever you set your mind to.

So, why do we tell ourselves so often in life that we *have* to do something? Why do we mentally position ourselves in a way to feel like we have no choice? Let's break free from our prison of "have to's" and enjoy the sense of freedom that comes along with feeling that we have our own agency, the power to choose.

"When you make a choice, you change the future."
~Deepak Chopra

We are in the driver's seat when it comes to our journey in life. We decide which way to go and we determine our destiny through our choices. This is something that successful people understand and implement. Empowerment comes from taking charge, deciding what you want and creating opportunities to get it.

Much of our behavior is shaped during the early years of our lives. Just think about it. When you were a young child there were probably lots of things that you wanted to do that you were not allowed to do, and more than likely you were told that you had to do certain things. For example, I remember being about 6 years old. My mom had just bought a new carton of Rocky Road ice cream, my favorite. I really wanted to eat the entire container, but my mom told me I couldn't. I was not allowed to do what I wanted to do. I remember the feelings of disappointment and helplessness that came when I was told I couldn't.

Now as an adult, I sometimes catch myself saying that I *have* to limit myself to a small bowl when I eat ice cream. In actuality, I have learned through experience that I *want* to limit myself so that I can be healthy. When I remember to use *want* instead of *have* in this frozen dessert scenario, I am more likely to stick to my choice because I feel like it is something I have decided. I feel empowered.

On the other hand, I was told by my parents, teachers and other adults that there were some things I had to do. I had to eat my dinner, clean my room or go to school. I felt like I didn't have a choice, but I did. I chose to do them because I didn't want to experiences the consequences of not doing them, but it still felt like the decisions were being made for me not by me. I internalized the message that I did not have a choice, I did not have any power.

Can you see how, as a young child, we often are told, or at least feel like, we can't have the things we want, and are conditioned to think that there are certain things that we "have" to do? What are the things you were told you couldn't do or have when you were younger?

The sense of feeling like you *have* to do things and can't do what you *want* spills over into your adult life. As an adult the stakes are higher—we aren't just dealing with ice cream and elementary school anymore.

Recently, I was speaking with client of mine who was struggling to find success in her business. I asked her what she was currently doing. She began reciting a list of items that she felt like she had to do to become successful. As she spoke I could see her shoulders start to slump with the weight of each task she was placing upon herself. I could almost feel her getting tired from where I was sitting across the room as she proceeded with her list of "have to's." The energy was seeping out of her. Not once did she mention the word want.

After she was done, I prompted her to rephrase her entire list out loud, replacing the word "have" with the word "want." Her body language and demeanor changed drastically. Suddenly she was full of energy. She sat up straight and scooted to the edge of her seat with eyes lit up, ready to go. She was excited and thanked me for reminding her why she wanted to begin her business in the first place, because she wanted to! She went from a place of helplessness to a state of empowerment!

When we *have* to do something, we feel helpless which sucks the life out of our passion and drive. It leaves us in a state of hopelessness, simply to be a victim of our own circumstances. I don't know about you but I don't want to be a victim. I want to be the master of my own life, determining what I want and creating the opportunities to get it.

Using or thinking the word *have* can literally drain your energy, whereas the feeling like you are doing the things you *want* increases your physical energy and power. It is energizing on so many levels. Occasionally I use muscle testing with my clients to prove this. In a nutshell, I apply physical pressure to an arm that is being held up to the side and they try to resist the pressure. When someone uses the word *have* in a phrase such as, "I have to be a good parent," the arm gets weak and the client cannot withstand the pressure. However, when I have them restate the phrase, replacing the word *have* with the word *want*, "I want to be a better parent," the arm remains strong.

Want is an empowering word.

Take the time to do the following experiment. Think of all the things in your life you have to do this week. Get a pen and a paper and start writing them down. How do you feel?

After writing your list of "have to's" you probably feel tired, a bit overwhelmed and low on energy. Maybe you feel helpless, a mere slave to your list of "to-dos."

Now, think of all the things you *want* to do. Write your list. How do you feel? You probably felt excited and may have even noticed a surge of adrenaline as you contemplated all those things you want. You probably feel empowered, hopeful and eager to manifest the things that you want.

Most of our "have to's" are really "want to's." We just aren't seeing them that way. If we can change our perception and self-talk, then we can change our energy surrounding what we accomplish each day. And, when we have more energy we will be more likely to get things done and we will move forward in life at an accelerated pace. People who view their daily tasks as daily desires, what they want to do, will find more happiness, peace and success throughout their lives.

I had a client that was describing to me that her major obstacle in life at the time was feeling extremely overwhelmed. Upon further questioning, I discovered that each day she would give herself a 5-page to-do list. She never completed every task on the list. She went to bed each night feeling guilty, tired and dreading the next day and the next daunting to-do list.

I introduced the *want* principle to her. But, instead of having her change every task on her unrealistic long list from have to want, I gave her a simple formula for success. It is one that I use and it is so empowering!

Each night before bed, I meditate or pray about what I might want to do the next day. I think about how to use my God-given gifts and talents to fulfill my divine potential. I don't expect an answer. In fact, I go to sleep without one. When I wake up the next morning, almost very first thing, I grab the paper and pen I keep by my bed and write down the first three things that I *want* to do that day. Sometimes they are career focused. Other times they involve things that I may want to accomplish that day as a mother or wife.

I only have three things on my list and they are all things that I want to do. I feel like that is a very reasonable amount of tasks. Almost every day I complete all three things and can go to bed feeling like I am successful. That does not mean that I only limit myself to those three things. But, I find that I always get more accomplished when I don't feel overwhelmed. I am significantly more productive and empowered to get more done since I have shifted from a long *have*-to-do list to my simple list of three things I *want*-to-do.

One important thing to remember when you are shifting your mentality from living a life of "have to's" to "want to's," is knowing what kind of life you *want* to create. Many people get so stuck in the rut of helplessness that they fail to think about what it is they desire. Perhaps this is done subconsciously, as a self-preservation technique. After all, who wants to dream about what they want when they don't feel empowered to get it? But, if you do decide to empower yourself by choosing to step out of victim mode and change your mentality, it is helpful to think about where you want to go in life.

Often times, I will have clients write down the story of where they want to be in a year from now. I did this at a time in my life where I felt like I had very little choice. I was stuck in the "have-to" mentality.

At the time, I was struggling financially. My job was okay, but I hated the hours. I felt like I had to work just so my kids could eat. I thought very little about what I wanted because all my energy was spent doing what I felt like I had to do just to survive. I felt very helpless and did not see a light at the end of the tunnel. I was stuck in the day-to-day grind of life, and it was wearing me down.

It was during this time that I was introduced to a mentor and made what I felt like was a huge sacrifice to pay less than $100 to attend his seminar. (Since then I have discovered the importance of mentors and have invested tens of thousands of dollars into hiring and working with them.) At the event I was given a long-term vision map and encouraged to think about what it was that I wanted my life to look like in the future. I was instructed to write the story of my future in present tense. So, I did. For the first time in years, I thought about what I wanted for the future. It was a bit scary. I wrote about what I wanted to manifest with my money, career, family, friends, community, spirituality and many other categories. I got really specific about what I wanted. The whole time I was thinking, "yeah, right!" I was afraid to allow myself to dream, but I did it and then careful folded the paper and tucked it into my binder.

Fast-forward 3 years. I was preparing for a class that I was teaching and going through some old material in my closet. I opened a binder and a paper fell out. It was my future story that I had written. I opened the paper and read about the life I wanted three years ago. I read about being a successful business owner who was inspiring people all over the country. I read about the peace that came with having a financial cushion and about how my kids were able to not only get the things they needed, but several of the things they wanted. I read about being able to travel.

As I read my dream vision of what I wanted, a tear slipped down my cheek. I realized that everything that I had wanted had come to pass. EVERYTHING I had written on that piece of paper had manifested in my life. I was living the life I wanted to live, one I had thought was only a dream a few years earlier.

How did I manifest the things I wanted in my life? Is it as simple as just writing them down? Is it really as easy as just allowing ourselves to dream? Maybe it is. Maybe it is just a matter of taking the time to think about what we want and then putting it down on paper. When we allow ourselves to want, we allow ourselves to dream. Choose to want. Choose to dream. When you know where you want to go, you will make the choices that will lead you there.

"'Would you tell me, please, which way I ought to go from here?'
'That depends a good deal on where you want to get to,' said the Cat.
'I don't much care where,' said Alice.
'Then it doesn't matter which way you go,' said the Cat."
-Lewis Carroll, Alice in Wonderland

Are you going to live a life of have-tos, not really knowing where you are going, where you are going to end up? Or, are you going to decide where you want to go so that you can make the choices to get you there? The Cat is right. If we have no vision, no direction, nothing that we really want in life, then does it really matter where we go? We will walk through this journey of life and end up where we end up.

Part of Soul Intuition is learning to embrace your own power and acknowledge your wants.

To want something is often viewed as selfish. Many people have the false belief that to want success somehow makes them conceited or self-centered. For some reason when they feel like they have to do something there is a sense of self-sacrifice. And, being obligated is perceived as being noble. But, what is really being sacrificed is their own happiness and success.

The truth, my friends, is that it is selfish not to share your God-given gifts, talents and unique message with the world. You are here on earth at this time for a reason. You have been given the life experiences and capacity to make a difference in people's lives and to better the world around you. All you have to do is want it. Do you want to feel more empowered? Do you want to let go of feeling like a helpless slave to your own have-to-do list?

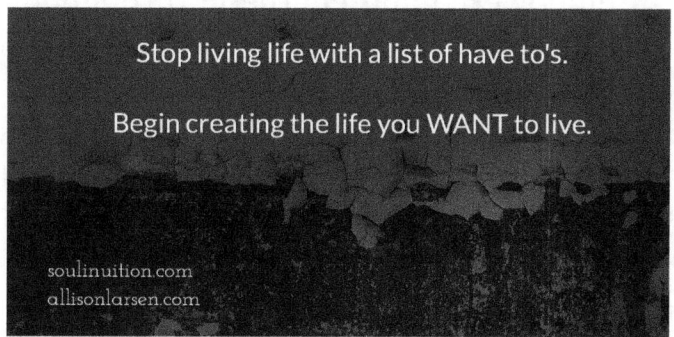

Your soul has a unique blueprint for success. You can discover it and learn how to use your God-given talents to build the life you are meant to live. The question you need to ask yourself is, "Do I want to?" If the answer is yes, then stop living a life of "have to's" and begin living the life you want.

So, how can you break out of this pattern? What can you do to start shifting the way you think, replacing have to's with want to's? The answer is simple, yet effective. You will begin to feel more empowered through the realization that your actions are a choice and nothing is forced upon you.

ACTION STEPS

1. Every time you catch yourself saying that you "have" to do something throughout the day, even if it is just in your mind, say the phrase out loud replacing the word *have* with the word *want*.
   - For example: If you catch yourself saying in your mind, "I have to go get gas," say out loud the following, "I want to go get gas!" You will feel more empowered and energetic throughout the day. As a result, you will begin to feel empowered to create the life you want.
2. Write down what you want for your future. Write in present tense and include family, financial, career, spiritual and personal goals. Go big or go home, as they say in Texas. It may be scary, but don't hold back.

Nothing can dim the light that shines from within.

~ Maya Angelou

5

Empowered to Shine: Becoming a Lighthouse

Dedicated to Cheryl, who has been a lighthouse for many.

We all have certain negative environments that we will find ourselves in, but even in these situations, we have a choice. We can be the victims of circumstance and allow the situation to define us, or we can embrace the challenge presented to us and grow from it. We can choose to be empowered or to be helpless.

When it comes to life, I see so many people living far below their potential, allowing whatever happens around them to define them. What they don't realize is that they have a choice. Just like my clients, Anne and Susan from a previous chapter, no one has a perfect life but we do have the power to define our experience.

You can be a lighthouse or a sponge. You always have a choice.

Let me explain what I mean. You can choose to be influenced by negativity or chose to be a positive influence on those around you.

I did not do a lot of housecleaning growing up and consequently was faced with a rather steep learning curve when I first was out on my own. I lived in an apartment with 5 other girls in a housing complex at a private college. A couple of times a month the manager would come around to do a cleaning check and the cleanest apartments would get rewards in the form of gift cards. As much as I disliked cleaning, the combination of having a very limited stream of income and a highly competitive nature motivated me to action. I quickly found that I seemed to be the only one in the apartment suffering from this motivation and as a consequence, would often be the one who cleaned the bathroom.

I had a little tote that contained a couple of cleaning products and some sponges. It was adequate and the bathroom would sparkle and shine after I got done. We often won the prize for the cleanest apartment.

One day the bathroom started to stink. It began as a musty undertone, but quickly developed into an undeniable and pungent stench. Eventually, I discovered its origin. Under the sink was my tote and inside was a bright yellow sponge I used to clean the toilets. I had not been properly rinsing and cleaning the sponge so it had absorbed all the icky toilet water and was now dotted with green. It had taken on the stench of the toilet and the bacteria, too!

Do you ever feel like you are a sponge, absorbing all the ick in the world around you, being influenced by the energy in your environment? If a family member is upset, you get upset. If your boss is having a bad day, you are having bad day. Your environment and the people around you influence how you feel. This works out great if you are always around happy people and reside year round at Disneyland. Otherwise, it can stink even worse than the sponge in my college apartment.

Now you may be asking yourself, "What is wrong with feeling sad or hurt when someone I care about is hurting?'

There is nothing wrong with feeling sympathy, or even empathy. But, there is a difference between identifying with someone's pain and taking on their emotions. We cannot take someone's sorrow from them, they have to work through it. When we allow their pain and sorrow to become ours, we become the sponge – absorbing the ick until all we can do is magnify the stench.

How often have you said to yourself, "I am having a bad day because my boss was grumpy, my husband was frustrated, or my daughter was mean." That is a lot of power to give others, a lot of power that is placed outside of ourselves. The more power we give away, the less empowered we become. Basically, we are giving up the choice to make our day, week, month or life what we want it to be. We are also giving up the opportunity to be an example or influence to those around us, to show them that life is what we make of it, not what others determine for us.

As a mother, I know that it is my responsibility to teach my children proper behavior. But children, particularly small ones, do not operate according to plan. We might be in the grocery store and my child decides to have a tantrum on the floor, or goes around knocking items off the shelf, or screams in the check out line because he wants a candy bar. I might get upset with the child and say something

I shouldn't, or maybe I make the situation worse by yelling at the child. I leave the situation feeling like a "bad" mom. I have placed that negative label on myself. I have allowed my circumstances to define me.

On the other hand, I could choose to remember that I am blessed to be a mother to my wonderful children and that there is a reason that they have been placed in my care. When they act out, I can choose to remain in control of my actions and remember that this may be a learning opportunity for them and for me. I can speak quietly to get their attention. At home when they are throwing a fit about cleaning up, I can make a game of picking up the items. If they get restless or bored and act out, I can help them think of a different activity or game, like taking out the dress up clothes. I can also examine what I have expected of the child, perhaps I have been expecting her to sit still for too long during errands and her body needs time to run around, or perhaps my child is tired because she is starting a growth spurt and her body needs more rest. Now I am in a position where I can learn what they need, rather than letting their poor mood influence me. I can channel the frustration of a cranky child into a learning opportunity for me.

We must choose to act by learning to shed even the smallest light from within as we find ourselves in negative situations. This may seem like a small thing, but the lesson is a powerful one. Darkness does not prevail against even the smallest light. When we react to negative behavior, we are choosing to keep ourselves in the dark. I will address acting vs. reacting to a greater extent in a later chapter.

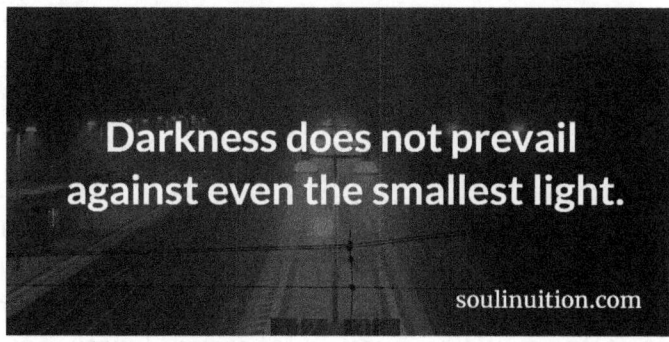

A lighthouse is constructed in such a manner that a small light is magnified and shines brightly to help show the way for others. Similarly, God has blessed you with light and He will bless you as you share that light with others. The key is to make sure that our light is always shining.

How do we make our light shine? There is so much good in the universe, so much love and so much light. All we need to do is magnify that light, that goodness, that love. We can radiate positivity and love once we tap into that source of never-ending light. We can be a guide to others as we share our gifts and the things we have learned from past experiences and lessons.

My husband always says there are two ways to learn, from counsel or consequence. We can shine our light as we take the time to share our counsel with others about our life lessons, so they have the opportunity to learn from us and not make the same mistakes we did. We can choose to shine, guiding others that cross our path with the light that we are emanating.

Or, we can keep our light dim. We can let fear stop us from magnifying our light and guiding others. We can choose not to fulfill our potential. We can choose to let our trials become obstacles instead of lessons and we will remain in the dark.

I remember a beautiful lighthouse my husband and I saw on a recent trip to Kauai. It was noble and tall, constructed on a beautiful peninsula that stretched out into the ocean, like a finger pointing the way. It was broad daylight and we could see it from miles away. However, later that night as we drove past the same location it was dark and if we hadn't have already seen it earlier in the daylight we never would have known it was there. The light was not on.

Upon further research, I learned that the light had not been on for nearly 30 years. When it was in operation the beam would stretch up to 90 miles away, serving as an important guide in the past for ships sailing to and from the Orient. I felt disappointed that I would not get to see this incredible beacon. It seemed to me like the lighthouse was not fulfilling its purpose, what it was created to do.

We can choose to be a beacon of light or we can be like the dark lighthouse. The flame may seem small, but as you magnify it with your God-given gifts that small flame will turn into a powerful beacon of light, cutting through the darkness in the world today helping others find their way. Small acts and simple things can be magnified into something great. God has blessed you with light and He will bless you as you share that light with others. In fact, the more we are willing to share our light, the brighter it will become.

A while ago I saw an inspirational story on Facebook about a high school boy named Josh. (WestJet, 2014) He had lost his father at an early age and missed him dearly. He had pictures of his father in his locker and the kids at his school would make fun of him for it. He felt isolated, alone and unloved.

In an act of desperation to save her son from a downward spiral of depression and isolation, Josh's mother moved him to another school. The hope was that a new beginning would make a positive impact.

Josh decided he wanted a different experience in his new school so he decided to hold the door open for people as they walked into the school. It was a simple gesture and at first most of the students thought it was a bit odd. But, as the weeks went on, they grew to appreciate the simple act of kindness and others started to join in, holding doors open for their fellow students in other areas of the school.

At the end of the year, Josh was voted prom king and given a door signed by every student in the school. It was an honor and Josh beamed with happiness, but he wasn't done making a difference. He decided that he had an important message to share with others so he became a motivational speaker, traveling to schools to talk to kids about bullying. Today, he is making a huge difference.

Josh is a lighthouse. He did not let his environment or circumstances define him. He decided to let his small light shine and over time it made a huge impact.

"The more you lose yourself in something bigger than yourself, the more energy you will have."
~Norman Vincent Pearle

Each of us has a light, a purpose, a calling in life, if you will. It may not be the same for everyone, but if we choose to find a way to make a difference and magnify it, we will be able to influence the people around us.

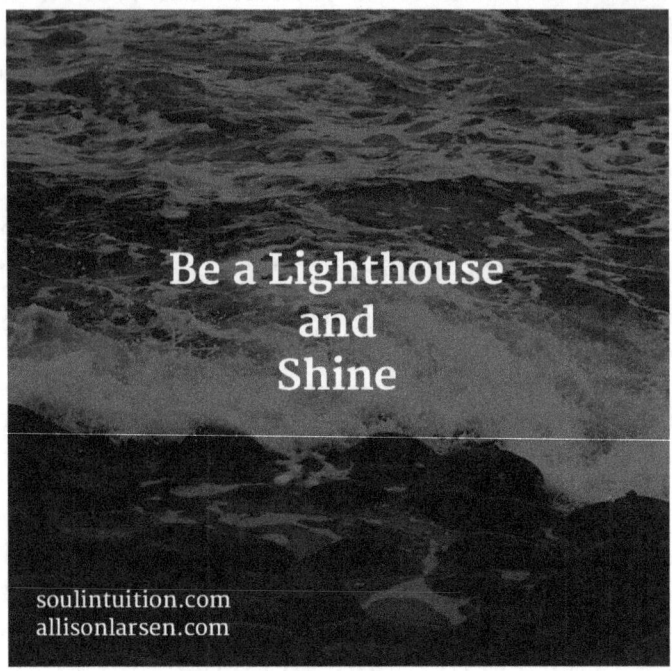

You can be a lighthouse for others, helping them find the path to greater happiness, and along the way you will find that your light has grown stronger.

So, the choice is yours. Will you be a sponge or a lighthouse?

Action Steps

1. Each morning when you wake up, decide how you want to feel and act that day. Come up with one emotion word to describe it, such as "happy."
2. Keep a pen and paper by your bed. After you determine your word for the day, write it down along with one thing that you can do to radiate or magnify that emotion in your life and the lives of those around you. This may come in the form of an act of service, an uplifting conversation or even an inspirational social media post.
3. Throughout the day think of your word and notice when you are being a sponge and when you are being a lighthouse. The first step in making a change is to recognize the behavior as it is happening. Change your mindset as soon as you realize it.
4. Before bed, take a moment to record what you accomplished and how you felt throughout the day. This is an opportunity for reflection, not self-judgment or criticism.

Only by giving are you able to receive more than you already have.

~ Jim Rohn

6

Empowered Through Giving: How Helping is Healing

Dedicated to Tiffany and Ann who have taught me the power of giving.

Giving is one of the most healing practices I have ever experienced and it is one I suggest to my clients all the time. I have seen people with intense emotional challenges, physical struggles, or terrible circumstances completely change by learning to focus on what they can give rather then what they don't have.

I remember a time in my life when I was struggling. In 2007, my husband and I had just built a new house. It was a stretch financially but the market had been good and we were able to do a lot of our own work so we planned to flip it and figured we could handle the steep mortgage for a short amount of time. He was in the construction industry and things had been booming.

Then, as the market crashed, so did our dreams. Everything we had planned on happening was not happening. We were stuck with a sky high mortgage and were upside down in the house. I had a personal training business that was very young and on top of that took a job managing a gym, but it wasn't enough. We still did not have enough money.

I was gone a lot from my family. I liked what I did, but hated being gone. Each night I would come home exhausted. Although we were both working, our savings was quickly being depleted. Our once large financial cushion was no longer there. In the summer of 2008, we cashed in our 401K just so our kids could eat. By that fall, I was discouraged and my husband was depressed. We tried to put on a happy face for our kids, but the truth was we were miserable.

During our financial abundance a few years prior, our family had started a Thanksgiving tradition. Each year we would look for a family in need in our community and provide all the fixings for a Thanksgiving dinner. We would fill a box with a turkey, potatoes, gravy, stuffing, pies, and homemade rolls and then drop it on their porch, ring the doorbell and run!

When we began this tradition, it was a relatively small financial sacrifice and the initial purpose was really to help teach our children about serving others. As Thanksgiving approached in 2008, I had no intention of carrying on this tradition as we were struggling just to feed our family.

One November evening we were all sitting in the living room together when our daughter asked who we were going to buy a turkey for this year. My husband and I looked at each other and I knew we were thinking the same thing.

How could we explain to our children that we had so little? I ignored the question and quickly changed the subject.

But her inquiry haunted me. As I lay in my warm bed later that night beside my loving husband in our safe home, sleep eluded me. I began to think about others around me who had less. Sure, we were struggling to make ends meet but we were doing it. Our kids had food every day and we lived in a nice home at a time when many of our friends had lost theirs. I had a loving family to come home to every night. I thought of a recently divorced lady in our church who had just lost her son in a car accident. I had my health. My mind reflected on a neighbor down the street who was bed-ridden, fighting a battle with cancer. As I thought about how blessed I was to have my home, my family and my heath, I felt something stir in my chest. For the first time in months I began to feel gratitude.

I awoke the next morning with a smile. This was a change. For the past few months, each morning I woke and just wanted to pull the covers over my head, hiding from my harsh reality. That day I sprang out of bed and started humming as I fixed breakfast. My husband and kids came down and the good mood seemed contagious. By the end of breakfast we were all laughing and happy.

My husband and I spoke later that day and decided we would carry on our tradition. It would be a sacrifice, but we were so blessed. We choose a lady from our church who was a single mom with a young daughter. She was suffering from back problems and was out of work. She and her daughter lived in a small, poorly furnished apartment. We all were excited the night we dropped off the box and ran. Our spirits were lifted and it felt good to help someone and expect nothing in return.

The next week I was in church with a group of people and among them was the single mom. We were discussing Christ's example of service. With tears in her eyes, this sweet woman told us that she had been feeling depressed and discouraged just prior to Thanksgiving. She wondered if anyone cared about her and in desperation had kneeled down and cried out to God, asking Him if He cared about her.

The very next day she received a knock on her door. When she opened it, she found a box with all the trimmings needed for a Thanksgiving dinner. She said in that moment she felt loved and knew God cared about her. It changed her life and she didn't know who did it but she would be forever grateful.

It was all I could do to keep from weeping. I dismissed myself and went to my car. I sat and sobbed. I had so much. I felt so blessed. The sacrifice we had made to provide that dinner seemed so small compared to the vastness of the warmth that surround me as I recalled her words. That experience changed me. My circumstances remained the same for a while, but my attitude was different. I was different. I was happy and felt gratitude on a daily basis. I never knew how much healing could come from helping someone. My life was changed. I thought that I was helping someone else and not expect anything in return. What I found was that I was the one that had been healed.

"No one has ever become poor by giving."
~Anne Frank, *The Diary of Anne Frank: The Play*

I love the Bible scripture that tells us to "love thy neighbor as thyself." I used to think this verse only meant that we should serve and show charity to our fellow men. What

I have come to learn is that there is an additional, less apparent meaning. When we help others, we will find healing ourselves.

You may be thinking that this sounds nice in theory, but where is the proof?

In fact, research has shown that people who volunteer are healthier, happier and generally more successful in life. Mark Snyder, a psychologist and head of the Center for the Study of the Individual and Society at the University of Minnesota said, "People who volunteer tend to have higher self-esteem, psychological well-being, and happiness. All of these things go up as their feelings of social connectedness goes up, which in reality, it does. It also improves their health and even their longevity."

When you take the time and effort to care and serve someone else, a beautiful thing happens. You become connected. You act as a divine servant, not only creating a bond with the person whom you are serving, but also with God and the universe. Connections to others and to God enable us to love, both to give it and to receive it. Love is healing.

"We can all reduce our life to a description that makes people feel sorry for ourselves or we can expand our life to a dimension where we can connect and give to others."
~Tony Robbins

If your soul is hurting, help someone. If you are sad, help someone. If you want something to be different in your life, then make a difference. We must help to the extent that we want to be healed. If we learn to help to match or even exceed the amount of pain in our lives, then we will experience true healing.

You may be wondering how someone measures how much help they need to give in order to heal. The formula is actually quite simple. Just add in sacrifice.

Helping + Sacrifice = Healing

Recently, I was listening to an inspirational talk given by Cynthia Kersey, creator of the *Unstoppable Foundation*, part of Tiffany Peterson's Gratitude Series. She said something that really struck me. "When you have a pain in your life, find a purpose greater than the pain." Sacrifice is simply suffering with a meaning, creating a purpose in the midst of our own pain. When we do that, our soul's focus will shift from the pain to the purpose. (Kersey, 2015)

For example, giving Thanksgiving dinner to a family in need was a nice gesture when we could afford it. I felt good afterwards and I had that "high" we experience from giving. But, when donating a Thanksgiving dinner was a sacrifice, when I had to really give up something to help someone else, that is when I found true healing for my soul from my own hopelessness and helplessness. I was blessed enough to hear how much that dinner meant to the recipient, but it wasn't necessary for my healing to take place. The healing began the moment I started the process, the train of thought that started that night my daughter asked the question led me to experience a measure of gratitude that was then magnified by the doing.

If you are wondering where to start, you must begin with your thoughts. If you are stuck in the process of always thinking about yourself, or what is not right in your life, you will not be motivated to give to others, which requires thinking outside of your world and stepping out of the "woe is me" victim mode.

Begin by thinking about those in your family, friend circle, neighborhood or church who may be suffering. Pick one person or family that comes to your mind and then think about what you can do for them. As you keep them in your thoughts throughout the day, you will find that your Soul Intuition will guide you to finding a way to help them. Remember, it doesn't always have to be a huge act of service, a big financial commitment, or hours of your time. Sometimes you can give hope, comfort or reassurance through a simple text or phone call. That is a great place to start.

The power of thought is amazing. Recently, I had an experience that shook me to the very core and rocked my world. I experienced a lot of pain surrounding this life lesson so in order to help myself heal, I decided to give a substantial amount of money to an organization that helped people in Africa. I felt so blessed and it helped my heart to heal as I received letters from one of the families helped by my donation.

I decided right there and then that I wanted to help and serve people in third world countries in person. I did not see how this would come to pass, but I started thinking about it. I included this desire to serve people in less fortunate areas of the world in my life story, a recording I listen to every morning all about what I want to manifest in my life. Within just a week of adding that piece to my recorded story, I was invited to go to India on a speaking engagement. The next day, I was invited to go to Africa on a humanitarian service trip!

Thoughts lead to actions. Actions create habits. Habits make your life. If you want to serve, think about serving first. If you want to give, think about giving. If you want to help, think about helping. You will attract the things you are thinking about. As you attract opportunities to help others, you will help yourself heal.

Mother Teresa said, "At the end of our lives, we will not be judged by how many diplomas we have received, how much money we have made or how many great things we have done. We will be judged by, 'I was hungry and you gave me something to eat. I was naked and you clothed me. I was homeless and you took me in."

Now, I am not saying that you should sell everything and donate all you have to the local homeless shelter. What I am saying is that if you want to heal the areas of your life in which you are struggling, make a sacrifice to help someone in need. Once you have changed your thoughts to focus on helping, do not wait until you have more. That faulty thinking will stifle your soul. Think about who you want to become and then help as if you are already there. If you want to be a person with financially sound resources that donates to local charities, than start donating to local charities even if you are not financially sound. You will find that other areas of your life will shortly match the frequency and intensity to which you are currently willing to give.

It is quite simply the law of attraction in action. We will become a result of who we are and of what we are doing today. If you would like to heal, then help. Helping is truly healing for the soul. Empower yourself to heal through giving.

> "Those who are the happiest are those who do the most for others."
>
> ~Booker T. Washington, Up from Slavery

Action Steps

1. Write down a list of items you would like to heal. For example, feelings of hopelessness, helplessness or worthlessness. Dig deep and come up with emotions that have been causing you real pain.

2. Start thinking about how you can help. Think about the people in your family, friend circle, neighborhood or church who could use some help. Remember, it all begins with your thoughts.

3. Decide how you want to put those thoughts into action. You will know it is a sacrifice when you start to question if you really can afford to do it. I am not just talking about monetary things. It could be a sacrifice of time, talents or resources. For example, to one person giving a $20 donation to a local church could be a huge sacrifice. For another person that may just be pocket change. Maybe for you donating 1 hour a week at the local food bank is a sacrifice in your busy life. Find a sacrifice big enough to equal your pain and you will experience healing for your soul.

Part 3
E<small>MBRACING</small> L<small>OVE</small>

The true secret to intuitive living is loving yourself enough to listen.

~ Allison Larsen

Every human being is the author of his own health or disease.

~ Swami Sivananda Saraswati

7

Loving All Layers: Healing from the Inside Out

Dedicated to Amber who first taught me to heal from the inside out.

We all deserve to be well, to be healthy and to be loved. These are not things we need to earn and we don't need to prove ourselves. We are divine beings with unique gifts, talents and purpose. There is nothing inadequate about us. The only limits are those placed on us through ignorance or the doubts and fears that we place on ourselves. One thing that has helped me to embrace my potential and love myself is learning how my soul functions. Knowledge is power, because when we understand something we are empowered to change it.

When I first learned and applied the principles I am about to teach you, my life changed. I was empowered to create the life I wanted, because I understood how my soul worked, how my body and spirit worked together to manifest the things I was creating through my thoughts. If you want to change your life, you must begin with your thoughts. Thoughts lead to actions. Our actions create our habits, and our habits make up our life. Now, I am able to recognize faulty thinking before it manifests in my life. If you are ready to completely embrace your power and learn to love yourself, raising the frequency around you and attracting abundance, then fasten your seat belt. Away we go.

There are four levels, or layers, to health and healing: spiritual, mental, emotional and physical. They are all interconnected and each plays a specific and important role in our overall well-being. To find true peace, happiness and healing we must acknowledge and learn to love ourselves on these four layers. It is only then that we will be able to fully recognize and embrace our God-given gifts and fulfill our divine potential.

Let me give you an example of how all four play a role in our health.

The Spiritual Layer

When I was a child, I remember watching a Tom and Jerry cartoon. For those who aren't familiar with iconic characters, Tom is a cat and Jerry a mouse that live in the same house and are always at odds with each other. In this particular episode, Tom agreed to behave while his owner was gone. But, as soon as she left he was tempted to chase Jerry, a decision that he knew would break his promise. While he agonized over what to do, an angel suddenly appeared on one shoulder and a devil on the other. The angel reminded Tom of his promise and gave him some positive encouragement by telling him that he was a good cat deep down. The shoulder devil laughed out loud after hearing the angel's argument and reminded him of all of his past mistakes, saying that he was really not a nice cat.

Eventually Tom chose to listen to the shoulder devil. Once he did, the angel disappeared and Tom began to chase Jerry. Eventually his owner came home and reprimanded the cat. He felt bad and regretted listening to the "bad" voice.

We, too, have "shoulder angels" and "shoulder devils" in the form of positive and negative influences all around us. We are constantly being bombarded with positive and negative messages and we get to decide which ones to listen to. These messages can come from media, other people, or sometimes just seem to be ideas that pop up out of nowhere.

We may hear that we are losers and can't do anything right. Or, we may hear that we are amazing with divine potential and that we can accomplish great things. These positive and negative influences have always existed. The positive messages around us come from God and are Truths. The negative ones are lies that become truth to us only when we start to believe them about ourselves.

This is the spiritual aspect or layer of health. It is good vs. evil, positive vs. negative, Truth vs. lie. It has existed since the beginning of the world.

THE MENTAL LAYER

Once we decide which influence to believe about our self, the positive or the negative, we enter the mental level. If we listen to the positive, we start thinking positive thoughts and when we listen to the negative our thoughts follow. For example, let's say I choose to listen to that shoulder devil who is telling me that me that I am not valuable or special. I begin to think thoughts like,

"I am a loser."
"I can't do anything right."
"I don't deserve to be loved."

On the other hand, let's say I choose to embrace the positive Truths. I begin to have thoughts such as,

"Using my divine gifts and talents, I can accomplish anything I put my mind to."
"I am capable of reaching my goals."
"I am lovable and am a valuable part of society."

Once we begin to entertain a thought, we have about 8 seconds to change that thought before the energy of it goes into motion.

Energy + Motion = Emotion

As I mentioned in the previous chapter, thoughts are so important because they really are the seed of the fruit we reap in life. The thought level is also the level where we can use choice. We can't always choose what thought enters our mind due to an external force or event, but we can choose whether to entertain that thought or not. Being able to control our thoughts will enable us to live the life we want. That does not mean we won't encounter difficulties. However, when we embrace loving, positive thoughts about ourselves we will live a life full of love and gratitude.

The Emotional Layer

What do I mean by thoughts creating energy in motion or an emotion?

Susan Reynolds explained it this way in an article in *Psychology Today*, "As far as your brain, every thought releases brain chemicals. Being focused on negative thoughts effectively saps the brain of its positive forcefulness, slows it down, and can go as far as dimming your brain's ability to function, even creating depression. On the flip side, thinking positive, happy, hopeful, optimistic, joyful thoughts decreases cortisol [a hormone associated with stress] and produces serotonin, which creates a sense of well-being. This helps your brain function at peak capacity." (Reynolds, 2011)

Thus, we can see how emotions really do stem from our thoughts. The chemicals released in our body are dependent on what thoughts we choose to entertain. These chemicals or emotions, the things we feel, actually create physical changes in our bodies.

Now, I am not saying that there will never be times that you feel negative emotions. After all, negative emotions are part of the human experience. It's what we choose to do with them that defines us.

For example, I may feel really disappointed if I don't get that huge speaking engagement for which I was being considered. I could choose to dwell on that disappointment, letting it develop into feelings of inadequacy. I may begin to think that I am not good enough or that there is something wrong with me and that must have been why I was not selected. I could let that inadequacy turn into a major roadblock preventing me from pursuing future speaking engagements.

Or, I could choose to allow myself to experience disappointment and then let it go. After using one of my favorite techniques of setting a timer for an allotted amount of time during which I give myself permission to fully experience negative emotions, I can choose to extend myself some love in the form of positive thoughts. I may choose to think about all the people I have been able to help. I may call a friend and ask for some encouragement, or I may take the time to participate in something I love to do. The key is to experience the emotion but not let it become your experience.

The other trick I teach my clients is to change their perception of a certain event that may have triggered a negative thought. Instead of looking at it as a trial, I teach them to look at it as an opportunity for growth and identify something they were able to learn from it. This allows them to feel a positive emotion surrounding the opportunity that was placed before them. We will learn how to do this in depth in the following chapters.

The fact is that what we choose to do with our emotions will affect us physically.

The Physical Layer

Many physical diseases stem from negative emotions. Let's take stress for example. Stress, by definition, is an emotion or a feeling with very real physical side effects. When you feel stressed out, cortisol, the stress hormone, is released into your body. What does cortisol do?

According to an article published by the Mayo Clinic, "When you encounter a perceived threat – a large dog barks at you during your morning walk, for instance – your hypothalamus, a tiny region at the base of your brain, sets off an alarm system in your body. Through a combination of nerve and hormonal signals, this system prompts your adrenal glands, located atop your kidneys, to release a surge of hormones, including adrenaline and cortisol.

Adrenaline increases your heart rate, elevates your blood pressure and boosts energy supplies. Cortisol, the primary stress hormone, increases sugars (glucose) in the bloodstream, enhances your brain's use of glucose and increases the availability of substances that repair tissues.

Cortisol also curbs functions that would be nonessential or detrimental in a fight-or-flight situation. It alters immune system responses and suppresses the digestive system, the reproductive system and growth processes. This complex natural alarm system also communicates with regions of your brain that control mood, motivation and fear." (Mayo Clinic, 2013)

This can be good during a short-term crisis, but if our bodies remain in this stressed state over a long period of time the cortisol can significantly decrease our immune system, leaving us susceptible to all kinds of disease.

"The body's stress-response system is usually self-limiting. Once a perceived threat has passed, hormone levels return to normal. As adrenaline and cortisol levels drop, your heart rate and blood pressure return to baseline levels, and other systems resume their regular activities.

But when stressors are always present and you constantly feel under attack, that fight-or-flight reaction stays turned on.

The long-term activation of the stress-response system – and the subsequent overexposure to cortisol and other stress hormones – can disrupt almost all your body's processes. This puts you at increased risk of numerous health problems, including:

- Anxiety
- Depression
- Digestive problems
- Heart disease
- Sleep problems
- Weight gain
- Memory and concentration impairment" (Mayo Clinic, 2013)

All that energy has to go somewhere. If we don't learn to recognize negative emotions and process them, they will manifest physically somewhere in our lives. Each layer of our being is connected. The spiritual influences the mental. What we choose to think about causes emotions. Our emotions manifest physically in our lives. Once people learn that these layers are connected, they can move past feeling inadequate and learn to love themselves. They realize how much choice they actually do have in their own health and well-being. I have helped many people go from feeling like helpless victims of their circumstances, thoughts and emotions to empowered individuals who are creating the life that they want to live because they don't let negative thoughts and emotions influence their lives.

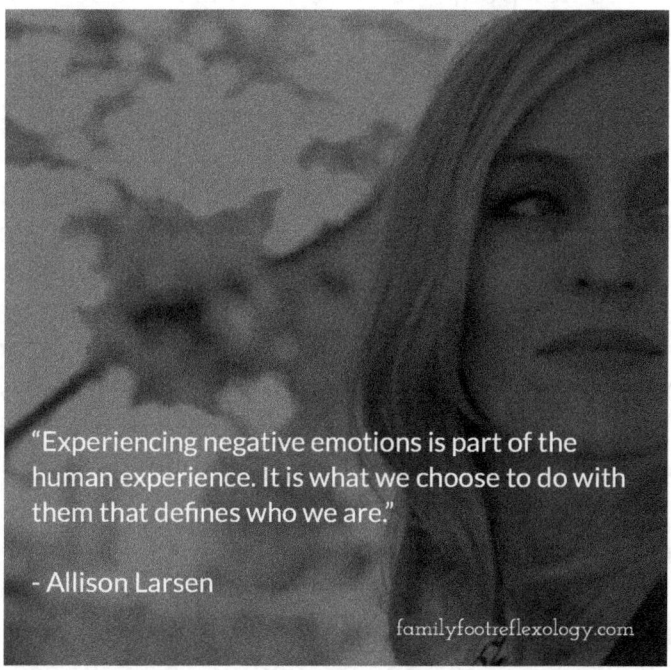

"Experiencing negative emotions is part of the human experience. It is what we choose to do with them that defines who we are."

- Allison Larsen

familyfootreflexology.com

Years ago, I was able to meet with a friend of mine who was suffering from terrible digestive problems. I offered to come meet with her and give her a foot zone. She politely brushed me off as she was meeting with several specialists that week that she hoped would be able to help her find answers. I told her I would keep her in my prayers.

A few weeks later, she posted a desperate plea for help on Facebook. She explained that she had spent tens of thousands of dollars on various medical specialists and treatments and she still had no answers. The pain was getting worse and she was spending large portions of the day literally screaming into her pillow in pain. She felt like a helpless victim to her physical pain and discomfort.

I replied to her post with two words. Foot zone. My friend called me almost immediately and I went to her house the next day.

The amazing thing about a foot zone is that it consists of over 120 reflex points on the feet. These reflex, or pressure, points work with the autonomic nervous system to help engage the parasympathetic or sympathetic system depending what the body needs. It also works off the meridians, which are energetic highways that run throughout the body. During a foot zone, I am not only able to identify physical blocks in the body based on the points in the feet, I can also recognize energetic or emotional blocks.

How is this done?

Research shows that people with similar physical diseases feel similar emotions preceding their illness or disorder. For example, Dr. Susanne Babbel wrote, "Studies have shown that chronic pain might not only be caused by physical injury but also by stress and emotional issues." She goes on to explain that, "often physical pain warns a person that there is…emotional work to be done." (Babbel, 2010)

Positive or negative spiritual influences inspire thoughts which trigger emotions which manifest physically.

There is a wonderful book I use in my practice to help people correlate the physical with the emotional called *Feelings Buried Alive Never Die* by Karol K. Truman. The last section of the book acts as an emotional reference guide with physical diseases listed in alphabetical order. Under each ailment is a list of emotions that people commonly feel when struggling with that particular physical challenge.

When I met with my friend, I was expecting that the points on her feet relating to the digestive system would be sensitive and have triggers, which they did. But, interestingly enough her elbow and hip points were also very sensitive. She was surprised and said she did not have any elbow or hip problems, but I had her look up the emotions related to those spots, explaining that maybe the triggers were emotional and not physical. As she read the description, tears filled her eyes and began to spill over, wetting her cheeks. The emotions she identified with were those having to do with major decisions and feeling conflicted. When she could finally speak she confirmed that indeed those were the very thoughts and feelings with which she had been struggling. She had been feeling a lot of pressure from the people around her about recent career opportunities and her role as a mother. She had begun to doubt herself and her choices. When I asked her if she had ever experienced this in the past she said that indeed she had, and had also struggled with similar physical issues at that time as well.

I walked her through an exercise to release the negative emotions and replace them with positive ones, which I will describe at the end of this chapter. I also helped her create some affirmations, or sayings, that she could use daily to begin to retrain her brain to think thoughts that would create positive energy. The next day she called me and said she was better. Three years later, she has not experienced a reoccurrence of symptoms.

When my friend confronted the doctors about how she had found relief from her constant pain they simply said that it must have been Irritable Bowel Syndrome aggravated by stress and that since she had found a way to cope with her stress they weren't surprised that she was feeling better. My friend was floored by this response and asked why they hadn't suggested that $20,000 ago!

The problem is that there has been a disconnect between Eastern and Western philosophy when it comes to health and healing. Modern medicine is wonderful and there are many amazing benefits and advantages. Cures are being found all the time for life threatening diseases, lives are being prolonged and saved. But, many practitioners of Western medicine have been taught to only focus on curing diseases rather than healing the whole person.

We often hear phrases like,
"I am worrying myself sick."
"You are killing me."
"I feel like I am going to die."

Over time as we continue to entertain these thoughts and emotions, they will begin to manifest in our lives.

True healing deals with the physical, emotional, mental and spiritual layers of our soul working together. Traditionally, curing just focuses on one area and ignores the rest. For example, someone may be diagnosed with cancer and is treated. After years of intense chemotherapy, losing their job, having relationships suffer and enduring intense mental and emotional challenges, the person's cancer may go away. They are "cured." However, the emotional, mental and spiritual problems will remain if they are not addressed as well. The patient may be cured from the disease, but they still need to heal.

It is very empowering to learn how to connect the physical to the emotional, the emotional to the metal and the mental to the spiritual. We can literally change our physical state. One time I remember my knee was bothering me after playing basketball. I had not had previous knee pain. I looked up the emotions associated with knee pain and identified that I, indeed, had been feeling the negative ones described. I had been told by someone in authority what to do. Being the somewhat independent and stubborn person that I am, I did not want to accept, or "bow" to authority. Consequently, that negative emotion was residing in the knee area.

I took a moment to release these emotions through writing them down on a piece of paper. I then choose positive emotions I wanted to experience instead. Next, I created an affirmation or statement that I could say out loud every time I heard that negative message enter my brain. Thus, I retrained my brain to focus on the positive. Immediately my knee pain went away and I felt great.

Too good to be true? No.
Don't believe me? Try it.

This process works wonderfully, but does take some practice and you have to be willing to accept that sometimes the pain or disease will not simply vanish.

Our physical trials can be lessons that teach us things and help us progress towards our higher self. To connect with our soul, we have to be willing to listen. In order for us to be empowered to have greater health using this technique, we also must accept our responsibility in creating the problem. This is hard for a lot of people to hear, but it is true. If we choose to have negative thoughts that trigger negative emotions that manifest physically, we are accountable. Once we understand this, however hard it may be to digest, we have the opportunity to become victors over our own health, rather than victims.

Now, you may be thinking that not every physical trial or disease is a result of our spiritual, mental and emotional state. There are times when things happen beyond our control. But, we still have to recognize and accept that healing needs to occur on all levels. When a person experiences an injury or gets a disease, accompanying it are emotions, thoughts and opportunities for growth. We can still work on thinking positive thoughts and creating positive emotions that will allow our souls to be in a state that is conducive for healing. We can choose to grow closer to God during the struggle.

ACTION STEPS

1. Make a list of physical ailments or diseases that you are experiencing. Think about the emotions you were feeling at the time the ailment began. See if you can pinpoint the negative ones.
2. Once you have identified the negative emotions, trace them back to the negative thought that created them. Think of a positive statement to replace that thought.
3. Now, every time you begin to think that negative thought, replace it with the positive statement.

For example: Sue is struggling with constant headaches. When she journals about her headaches, she realizes that they began around the time she started her new job. She was feeling stressed and under a lot of pressure. She recognizes that she began thinking thoughts around that time such as, "I am so stressed out!" or "I am completely overwhelmed."

Sue realizes that she does not want to feel stressed and overwhelmed and that these thoughts may be causing negative emotions that are manifesting physically in the form of a headache. She decides she wants to feel peaceful and calm. So, Sue writes the following statement down, "I am peaceful and choose to remain calm throughout my day at work." Every time Sue begins to think about how stressed she is, she simply repeats the statement she created, replacing the negative thought with a positive one.

Weeds are flowers, too, once you get to know them.

~Eeyore (A. A. Milne)

8

A Loving Perception: Learning to See the Good

Dedicated to Riley, who has always seen the good in me.

Our perspective shapes our life. It is all about what we choose to see. Is it a weed or a flower? Is it a trial or a lesson? Is it a hardship or a gift from God? It is my belief that we can grow and learn from everything in life. We can choose to shed the chains of inadequacy that bind us and embrace self-love. We can turn stumbling blocks into stepping stones, allowing us to get closer to our divine potential simply by changing our attitude or how we view our situations and opportunities in life.

I want you to think of something in your life right now that is a trial. Maybe it is a health challenge, a financial struggle or a relationship hiccup. Now, I want you to place that trial right in the palm of your hand and wrap your fingers around it. Keep it there while you read the following experience I am going to share with you. At the end we will look at that problem again.

I am going to tell you about the "worst" day of my life.

I was a young mother with 2 very young children and a third on the way. This third child was a surprise, meaning that I had become pregnant much sooner than we had planned. My oldest daughter was 3 and my youngest was just barely 1 year old. My husband had just graduated from school and he was working at his first job. We lived in a small upstairs apartment and were struggling to make ends meet, to say the least.

This particular day was dance class for my 3-year old. Despite our meager income I had decided that we could not forgo exposing our children to the arts and creating opportunities for them to develop their talents. So, since I had taken dance as a young child, I thought that would be the best for my daughter. The problem was that I had forgotten to consult with her. She hated dance. However, we had prepared for the class and since it was such a huge sacrifice for us, I dragged her to dance every Monday and Wednesday morning.

This day was particularly bad and I ended up practically carrying her down the cement stairs from our apartment with one hand and holding my baby in the other, all while sporting a very pregnant stomach and all of our gear. Exhausted, we finally arrived at her class, but she refused to participate. She sat right in the middle of the floor while the teacher tried desperately to convince her to either participate or at least move. As I watched from the parent's viewing window I felt discouraged and frustrated. To make matters worse, my baby was fussy.

I think one of the fellow dance moms could see that I was having a rough day and she came over to try to cheer me up, but failed miserably. She began with small talk, which was distracting in a good way at first until she started to tell me about an upcoming trip to the Caribbean that she and her husband had planned. I am sure she did not think this was out of the ordinary as I lived in an affluent area (except for our apartment building) and exotic trips were quite the norm for many. However, as she spoke of sun and sand and all the activities and amenities at the resort, all I could think about was how we could barely afford gas to drive across the state a couple of times a year to visit my family.

As class ended, I was glad to be done with hearing about vacations that were out of reach and looking forward to nap time for all of us. I was tired, and slightly depressed and all I wanted was to lay down, but my girls had different plans. Both refused to nap. Argh! After fighting to get them to lay down for about 2 hours, I gave up and turned my attention towards fixing dinner. It had been a while since my husband's last paycheck and as I looked through the cupboards all I could find to make dinner was a can of tuna and some stale bread. Tuna on toast…again. I hated tuna on toast.

As I made dinner, the baby was fussy and my oldest daughter was clingy. What should have taken 20 minutes, turned into an hour long fight to get food on the table. But, still no husband. Where was he? I couldn't wait for him to come home so we could eat. Then I could hand off the kids and put my feet up. As I waited and wondered, I grew more upset. Why was he so late?

After what seemed like an eternity, the phone finally rang. It was my husband, but his usual strong voice sounded weak. He explained that he had grown extremely ill throughout the day and had gone to a local clinic to discover that he had appendicitis and was going to the hospital for a routine appendectomy. He assured me that everything would be okay, but to find a sitter and meet him there. Seriously, this had to be the worst day of my life!

I didn't make it to the hospital in time to see my husband before surgery. I sat in the waiting room hungry, tired and worried as I thought about him and how in the world we were going to pay for all the medical bills. After several hours the doctor came into the room. "Mrs. Larsen," he said, "this is the luckiest day of your life." I almost laughed. He must be joking. Then he went on. "Your husband should have died on that operating table. It is a miracle he is alive." I was shocked. Wasn't this just a routine appendectomy?

The doctor explained that for some reason my husband's platelet count was extremely low and he should have bled to death. They would not have performed the surgery had they known. He said that none of the doctors in that room could explain why my husband was still alive. He should not have survived. Yet he did and it looked like he was going to be okay.

Suddenly, the worst day of my life was the best day of my life. I had my husband. I had my family. All the little things that had gone wrong throughout the day seemed so minor and inconsequential as I viewed my day through this new perspective.

For the next year, we fought a battle with ITP, a rare disease, which almost took my husband's life several times. It still may, someday. But, after the doctor told me I was lucky and I shifted my perception, I was grateful and peaceful throughout the rest of the ordeal. I committed to treat each day with my husband as a gift from that day forward.

What if we could look at all of our trials as gifts? Gifts from God to teach us. Lessons to help us learn what is important in life, what we are capable of and how many people we have who love and support us.

I see many clients who initially view themselves as victims of their circumstances, enduring the trials placed before them and struggling to get through. What a miserable life. This type of mentality stifles growth and learning. It is not only disempowering but, quite frankly, depressing. I don't think God or the universe is set up to stifle us, rather they are set up so we can succeed. We can choose to feel inadequate and unloved, or we can change our view and start flourishing. So, how can we go from merely surviving to thriving in our circumstances?

We need to change our perspective!

I firmly believe that each opportunity (notice how I didn't say trial) that is placed before us in this life is there so we can grow, so that we can become better versions of ourselves abounding in wisdom and light. As we grow and learn, we can share those life lessons with those around us, giving them an opportunity to learn from counsel instead of consequence. As we work to help others, our light will shine even brighter.

We are the lighthouse. The small spark that is magnified and shared.

Recently I went through a couple of months of extreme emotional, mental and physical pain. I was involved in a relationship that ended in heartbreak and pain. Shortly thereafter I was in a terrible snowmobile accident. I crushed my chest and got a concussion. I was prescribed narcotics and experienced an intense withdrawal when I decided I no longer needed them for the pain. This was my third concussion, and, as is common with multiple head injuries, I experienced some chemical imbalances that caused anxiety, OCD and severe depression. I had experienced anxiety and OCD before and although not pleasant, I knew what to expect. The depression caught me completely off guard. The cure was to let my brain heal by doing nothing and taking no medication. I literally felt as if I were trapped in my own hell.

It was in the midst of my darkest days that I was sent an angel. My friend Shelby visited me and said something so true that helped my to shift my perspective from a place of feeling inadequate and unloved to feeling love and gratitude for what I was experiencing.

"Allison," she said, "you are becoming an amazing guru. You are going to be able to better help the people with whom you share your message."

The meaning of *gu* is from darkness and the meaning of *ru* is into the light. I was experiencing the darkness so that I could more fully embrace the light.

I could use my experiences to really empathize with my many clients, friends and family. It wasn't long after that I was able to help my daughter with a difficult problem that she was experiencing by coming from a place of complete understanding, non-judgement and love. She said my reaction changed her life. As a mother, my entire two months of hell was all worth it if only for that.

I am so thankful for my friend. God places certain people in our path to guide us, to teach us, to love us, and to remind us of who we are and who we can become. These angels can help us shift our perspective. Whether we are inspired by a friend, a book or a motivational speaker, we can step out of inadequacy and into a space of love and learning as we change our perspective.

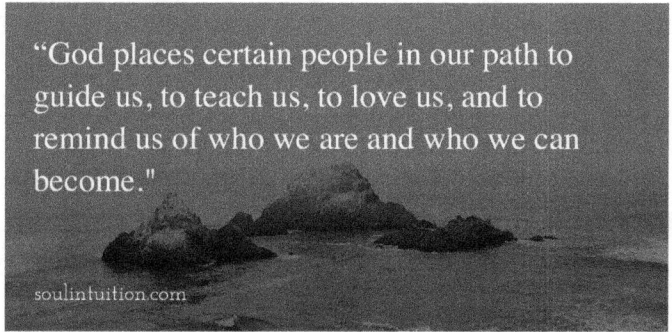

Here is a simple step that you can take towards shifting your perspective. Consider the trial I asked you to hold in your hand. Have you ever asked what you are supposed to learn from it, how it can help you grow? If you don't know the answer, ask God.

We have a choice. We can continue to grow and learn and progress towards our highest self in this life, or we can remain stuck. I choose to grow.

Think back to school. The whole education system is ideally set up to help us learn, grow and progress to a higher level of education. In order to progress however, we have to pass tests to prove that we have grasped a concept so we can move on to the next. Life is the same. Our trials are tests. Once we prove that we have learned what we need to learn, we can move on.

I love to watch hurdle races during the Olympics. The runners speed and agility and how they glide over each obstacle with grace and ease amazes me. In order to keep going in the race, each hurdle needs to be cleared. We can view our trials as hurdles. The longer it takes for us to get over each, the more time it will take for us to progress, to move on. Sure, we may encounter more hurdles, but if we keep going we are getting closer to the finish line!

There are some trials that we will not move on from in this life. We all know people who have died from a disease or struggle with life-long disabilities and health challenges, but we all can learn and move on the spiritual, mental and emotional levels.

Think back to my friend Anne that struggled with cancer. She did not let her disease define her. Although she had physical limitations that she struggled with, she chose to keep loving herself and her those around her. She chose positive emotions and she chose not to feel inadequate as a mother, wife or friend. She continued to feel loved and to love. She continued to think positively and she continued to progress with influencing those around her for good. She did not give up. She continued to develop her relationships. She continued her mental, emotional and spiritual progress even though her body was deteriorating. She continued to progress in the areas that were within her control.

There are many situations in which we may feel inadequate and even unloved as we struggle to understand why something is happening to us or someone we love. One of the most difficult challenges as a parent, spouse or friend is to see someone we love in pain or hurting. Maybe you have experienced watching someone you care about struggle. You may feel helpless and wrestle to comprehend that there is a lesson that could be learned by them and by you to help you both progress and grow.

A lady in one of my classes, Donna, shared a profound experience with me in which her perspective shifted in a rather drastic manner. One day she arrived home from work to find a message from her 20-year old son that he had been diagnosed with a life threatening disease. He had just moved out on his own and was living in San Francisco hundreds of miles away. His insurance was only valid in the state of California so he was stuck living there until his treatments were complete.

This mother described how she would fly back and forth from Idaho on a regular basis to help drive her ill son to the hospital and doctor appointments. She told how she and her husband went hundreds of thousands of dollars into debt from travel, accommodations and bills. She explained how indescribably hard it was as a mother to watch her son in pain. She watched her healthy self-sufficient son turn into a shadow of his former being, completely dependent on others. She would sit by his bed and watch him sleep, silently praying and asking God why this had happened. Often times she would travel alone, tag-teaming with her husband to make sure their son had constant care.

She told me how she questioned God in anger one night. "Why would you do this to my son?"

Finally, after years of sacrifice and struggle, her son got better and was able to move back to Idaho. Ten years later she was talking with her son and mentioned how the worst thing she had ever experienced in her life was almost losing him. Her son replied, "Oh mom, my disease didn't almost kill me, it saved me." He went on to explain how he had gotten in with the wrong crowd and was in a gang at the time he got sick. He was in deep, too deep to get out on his own. The only way out of the mess he found himself in with the gang was to be diagnosed with a life-threatening illness. He told her that he was sure he would be dead if he had not gotten cancer. Suddenly, her perception changed. She said she thanked God every day from that day on that her son had gotten sick. What she once thought was an unfair circumstance in which the universe and God were conspiring against her and her son, she now viewed as an amazing gift. She learned that not everything is what it seems and that growth can happen as we choose to look at things from a different view.

We can learn. We can grow. But to do so we need to have a greater perspective. We need to look at our lives as opportunities for growth. Many successful, influential and wise people have learned this lesson.

"When we are no longer able to change a situation, we are challenged to change ourselves."
~Viktor Frankl

Viktor Frankl was a holocaust survivor. He endured physical, mental, emotional and spiritual despair. During his time in the concentration camp, he had every reason to feel inadequate and unloved. Many around him were giving up all hope, but Frank chose a different perspective.

"We stumbled on in the darkness, over big stones and through large puddles, along the one road

A Loving Perception: Learning to See the Good   121

leading from the camp. The accompanying guards kept shouting at us and driving us with the butts of their rifles. Anyone with very sore feet supported himself on his neighbor's arm. Hardly a word was spoken; the icy wind did not encourage talk. Hiding his mouth behind his upturned collar, the man marching next to me whispered suddenly: 'If our wives could see us now! I do hope they are better off in their camps and don't know what is happening to us.'

That brought thoughts of my own wife to mind. And as we stumbled on for miles, slipping on icy spots, supporting each other time and again, dragging one another up and onward, nothing was said, but we both knew: each of us was thinking of his wife. Occasionally I looked at the sky, where the stars were fading and the pink light of the morning was beginning to spread behind a dark bank of clouds. But my mind clung to my wife's image, imagining it with an uncanny acuteness. I heard her answering me, saw her smile, her frank and encouraging look. Real or not, her look was then more luminous than the sun which was beginning to rise.

A thought transfixed me: for the first time in my life I saw the truth as it is set into song by so many poets, proclaimed as the final wisdom by so many thinkers. The truth – that love is the ultimate and the highest goal to which Man can aspire. Then I grasped the meaning of the greatest secret that human poetry and human thought and belief have to impart: 'The salvation of Man is through love and in love.' I understood how a man who has nothing left in this world still may know bliss, be it only for a brief moment, in the contemplation of his beloved. In a position of utter desolation, when Man cannot express himself in positive action, when his only achievement may consist in enduring his sufferings in the right way – an honorable way – in such a position Man can, through loving contemplation of the image he carries of his beloved, achieve fulfillment. For the first time in my life I was able to understand the meaning of the words, 'The angels are lost in perpetual contemplation of an infinite glory.' " (Viktor Frankl, Man's Search for Meaning)

Viktor chose to embrace love. He chose to shift his perspective and discover hope in even the most dire of circumstances. Consequently, he survived his ordeal and went on to touch millions of people with his inspirational messages.

"Character cannot be developed in ease and quiet. Only through experience of trial and suffering can the soul be strengthened, ambition inspired, and success achieved."
~Helen Keller

Helen Keller could have been little than a medical footnote about an unfortunate life. But, she choose not to let her circumstances define her. She choose to learn and to grow and to succeed despite every reason to feel inadequate. Helen learned to love herself and embrace her gifts. She inspired and touched millions with her positive perspective and view of life.

During a lecture Helen Keller gave, the Weekly Dunn County News reported, "The wonderful girl who has so brilliantly triumphed over the triple afflictions of blindness, dumbness and deafness, gave a talk with her own lips on "Happiness," and it will be remembered always as a piece of inspired teaching by those who heard it." (the Weekly Dunn County News, January 22,1916)

Shift your perspective. Embrace the gifts you have been given. Learn from your trials. Grow. Progress. Become. Like Hellen Keller and Viktor Frankl, shed the chains of inadequacy that bind you and love yourself.

Your soul will thank you.

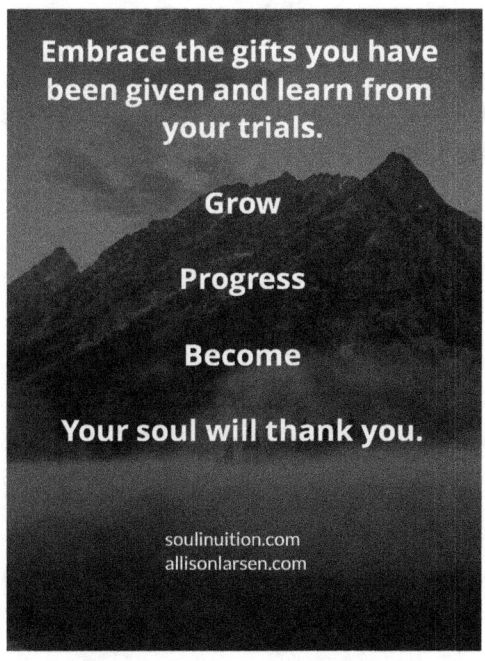

Action Steps

1. Fold a piece of paper in half hot-dog style.
2. On one side write down a list of your trials. On the other side write down the things you have learned or can learn from them.
3. If you are having trouble identifying what you can learn, spend some time in meditation. Clearing the brain can be an effective tool for letting go of our preconceived notions, creating an environment conducive to new ideas and a shift in perspective. For those of you new to meditation, simply begin by setting your timer for 10 minutes. Lay down in a comfortable position and relax your body and your mind, letting go of stress and tension. It helps to focus on your breathing and listen to calming music.
4. After completing the list, take a moment of gratitude for all the opportunities you have been provided, all the gifts God has give to you.

What would you look like if you saw yourself through the eyes of God?

~Oprah Winfrey

9

VISION OF LOVE: LEARNING TO SEE THE DIVINE WITHIN

Dedicated to Jennifer and Annette, who show me unconditional love.

What if you were asked to make two lists, one of your weaknesses and one listing all of your strengths? Which would be longer?

Many people have no problem reciting hundreds of flaws, but struggle to list off just a few good qualities or things they love about themselves. Or, how often at the end of the day do we reflect back, looking past all of the good things we have accomplished and magnify the one mistake or misstep we took?

I play the cello. It is a great creative outlet for me and I am fairly good. Years ago before I learned many of the tools I am sharing with you, I was asked to play at a funeral. When I play at funerals, I always want to do my best because I view it as a time to honor the person and their life. The funeral was nice, but different.

This particular day, I got there early to tune and set up my instrument so I would not disrupt the service. Although I did not know the individual, I stayed for the entire thing because mine was the last number. It was a piece I had played a hundred times. For the most part, it went well. However, there was one part I messed up on, one wrong note. I actually doubt anybody could tell except for my accompanist, but still, I was disheartened.

As I drove away from the funeral, I was feeling angry at myself and very disappointed. I began mentally beating myself up. I called my friend to complain, but she wouldn't have it. She reminded me that I had sacrificed my entire Saturday afternoon to help someone out, and here I was focusing on something that I did wrong for one second. It was so true! I am grateful for a courageous friend who was willing to point out the good when I was in the space of self-criticism and self-doubt over a tiny mistake.

How often do we do this to ourselves? How often do we overlook all the good things we've done and focus on the one thing we should have done, but didn't do or could have done better? When we reflect on our imperfections we feel less than adequate.

How do we move past our feelings of inadequacy?

The answer is to learn to see yourself through a divine filter. When God looks at us he sees our soul's potential. He focuses on what we have been given, not what we don't have. He sees our accomplishments and doesn't focus on our mistakes. God also recognizes those weaknesses that are preventing us from becoming all we can. But instead of allowing weakness to define our souls He knows we can learn and grow from them.

How do I know this? Because I have spent years practicing the art of seeing myself through the eyes of God. As I have done this, my ability to love myself has grown and my self-image is at a healthy level. When I look in the mirror, I see my potential and my gifts and I can celebrate my accomplishments. At times, I do make mistakes or give in to my weaknesses, but when this happens I now view myself with divine compassion and understanding. I do not waste time or precious energy beating myself up. I do not dwell on my mistakes nor allow them to define me or disable me. I am gentle with myself and I move on. It is a great way to live and it creates an environment conducive for me to tap into my Soul Intuition and recognize my God-given gifts and talents.

I did not always see myself through God's eyes. In fact for a large portion of my life I did what many people do, I focused on everything that was wrong with me. I could barely look at my own reflection because I would pick myself apart. I could only see my short-comings and constantly felt inadequate. It was a hard way to live and it prevented me from recognizing the many gifts and abilities I had that could bring me lasting happiness and bless the lives of many others. My self-image was truly stopping me in my tracks from reaching greatness and feeling like I was living my purpose.

For those of you stuck in self-hate, self-criticism and self-doubt, you are not alone. Many people live this way and it is a miserable way to live! What you are about to learn will enable you and empower you to make a crucial shift in your life. You will find that as you implement these steps you will recognize your divinity. You will find your true purpose and be able to embrace it. By so doing, you are working towards transcendence, the ability to feel like you are using your potential to change your life and better the world around you. At the end of the process you will feel fulfilled and with that comes a deep sense of peace and joy.

Sounds amazing doesn't it? So, where do we start? A motto of mine is that knowledge is power. When we learn about ourselves and understand what is happening within, we are able to recognize the things that are stopping us, release them and replace them with things that we want. Let's compare ourselves to a tree. Our behaviors regarding self-image are merely the fruit. We need to get to the root of the issue to make a true change. So, lets do some digging about our self-image.

There are typically two things that affect a person's self image: how you see yourself and your perception of how others see you.

How you see yourself

Our souls have perfect potential stuck in an imperfect body. But, dwelling on our flaws will only magnify them. They will become so big that we cannot move past them. I have worked with thousands of people all over the world and the number one thing I see standing in people's way from achieving all they could are their own feelings of inadequacy. We are severely limited by our own beliefs and perceptions. If we don't see ourselves as valuable, then we will not allow ourselves to be valued by others. If we believe that we are flawed and broken, then we will not be able to fix our relationships, finances or businesses. If we cannot see how we can be successful, then we never will be. It is as simple as that. Change your self-image and change your life.

I am not just talking about what is on the inside when it comes to image. Though some may feel it is shallow, the reality is that a large portion of how we view ourselves is dependent on how we feel that we look on the outside.

As a young mother, I struggled with self-image. I am naturally lean and lost weight quickly after having each of my children. But, all I could see every time I looked in the mirror were the pockets of fat that remained. The small amount of cellulite on the back of my thighs was barely noticeable, but I couldn't see anything else when I glanced at my legs. I could hardly stand my own image. In fact, for about a decade, my entire 20s, I would not stand closer than 5 feet to a mirror. I was horrified when I pulled down the visor mirror in the car because it was too close and all I could see was what was wrong with my complexion.

Instead of feeling beautiful I felt ugly. And, I let it affect my life. I became obsessed with what I ate. This obsession compromised my ability to focus on my relationships and talents and instead of growing, I was shrinking both literally and figuratively. All my energy was spent trying to fix what was wrong with my body, but it wasn't until I changed my perception and was able to love myself that my body image began to change.

Before I shifted my self-image, I would always require the lights to be off whenever my husband and I were intimate. I wouldn't stand very close to people when I spoke because I was afraid that they would notice my flaws. In fact, many people thought that I was stand-offish and cold. I would spend loads of time and energy getting ready before going to volunteer at my children's school because I wanted to look good for them.

It is important to understand why we may feel a certain way. For me, image was very important because I grew up with a dad who was a local celebrity. Wherever our family went, I felt like people were always watching us. Don't get me wrong, there were many perks and I loved being the center of attention most of the time, but the story I chose to create for myself was that people were very concerned with appearances and I was always being watched and judged according to how I looked. When I didn't feel like I looked perfect, then I felt like people wouldn't like me. When I finally recognized the false story I had created and embraced, I knew I needed to let that go. I needed to rewrite my story to one centered around feeling loved and beautiful. This new story changed my self image and I found that I was able to embrace my God-given gifts and move forward in using them to fulfill my divine potential.

Here is a brief example to illustrate my point. It is the story of the ugly rock.

Once there was a field of rocks by a crystal clear lake at the base of a beautiful mountain in the Northwest. Some rocks were big and some were small. Some were smooth and colorful and others were rough and grey. There was one rock that was particularly ugly. It was a nondescript tan color with large asymmetrical pores. Rough calcite formations were scattered about the surface. It was not very large and not very small. This rock was nothing special.

Occasionally hikers would come to the rock beds to search for beautiful pieces to add to their collections. The ugly rock would watch as girls and boys of all ages came. They would pass him by. The girls wanted something shiny and sparkly. The boys would often look for smooth stones to skip across the lake.

The ugly rock wanted more than anything to be normal instead of ugly. He wanted someone to choose him, to think he was special. But day after day he just lay there watching as other rocks around him were admired and desired to bring a little happiness and joy into someone's life.

One day the rock was enjoying the sun's warm rays when a shadow fell over him. He looked up and saw a man blocking the sun. He was old and not particularly handsome. His skin was rough with large pores and moles dotted his face.

He was neither large nor small. He wore a nondescript tan uniform.

The ugly rock thought he must be admiring the smooth black rock next to him. He had given up long ago on being noticed. And if he were to be noticed he decided he would want it to be a small girl with yellow hair. He liked them best.

To his surprise the man pick him up. He noticed how the warm skin of his palm felt like the sun under his rough exterior. The man brought him close to his face and smiled. For a moment the rock felt a surge of excitement. But that was short-lived. The man raised his arm high above his head and propelled him towards the ground.

In that split second before he crashed into the ground the rock thought many things.
"This man must have been so disgusted by my ugliness that he is throwing me away."
"I am worthless anyway."
"I deserve to be crushed."
"I was foolish to think that anyone would ever see beauty in me."
The rock felt the pain of crashing into the ground and everything went black.

When he awoke there was a group of spectators with mouths agape. He noticed that he had been split in half and the feeling was surreal, although not painful. One of the spectators, a beautiful young girl with long blonde curls exclaimed, "How beautiful!" as she picked up one of his halves. Another young man declared, "This is the most beautiful thing I have ever seen." as he picked up the other half.

The rock was confused and couldn't comprehend why they were speaking that way until later that evening. The blonde girl still held her half as she walked to the lake. As she bent over to admire the smooth surface of the water, the ugly rock caught a glimpse of his reflection and couldn't believe what he saw. On the inside there were beautiful purple crystals. He was a valuable geode!

He had always been beautiful. He just needed to recognize the greatness within. It was slightly painful in the moment, but so worth it! For what was uncovered brought beauty and joy to those around him. He made the world a more beautiful place.

How many us are like the rock—failing to see our own potential and only focusing on our flaws?

At this point you may see the importance of how you see yourself plays a role in your life, but you may be wondering how to determine your current self-image. Here is an easy way to gage if this is something that could be hindering you from reaching your potential.

Quiz
Take this simple quiz. Rate each statement on a scale of on 1-5 with 1 being very negative and 5 being super positive.

1. When you look in the mirror, you are happy with what you see.
2. After completing a project, you feel accomplished and can admire your work.
3. When you make a mistake, you don't dwell on it.
4. When you think of where you are in life right now, you feel happy.

5. Your internal dialogue is positive and self-motivating.

Most people's sum scores fall below 12. What was yours? If you are below 18, you are allowing how you see yourself to prevent you from living the life you were meant to live. Stop it! Begin today with positive self-talk.

Your perception of how others see you

The second thing that affects our self-image is our perception of how others see us. This is so true! Have you ever been paralyzed by fear of what someone may think of you?

"The eyes of others our prison, their thoughts our cages."
~Virginia Wolf

I have had the amazing opportunity of helping presenters and speakers all over the nation and I often see that what gets in the way of them doing their best, giving their all, and delivering their message is the fear of what the people in the audience think of them.
Am I wearing the right outfit?
Will they think I am too loud and pushy?
Will people think I am a push over?
Do I have a cliff hanger? (That one is a big fear of mine!)
And the list goes on and on.

I have seen teenagers that are so smart and have so much to give, absolutely refuse to participate in class for fear of what others might say or think of them. It is a shame when I see greatness stifled by fear.

When we learn how to quit wondering what others are thinking and focus that energy towards our life's mission and purpose, amazing things begin to happen. There is unparalleled power unleashed when one learns to speak from the heart and share their passions without reservation. Their message is freed from the cage of self-doubt and allowed to take flight into the hearts and souls of the people listening. Lives are changed, spiritual gifts are opened, and divine missions are financed with the wealth of courage and confidence that accompanies those who have freed themselves from the bonds of self-consciousness.

My study and experience with energy has helped me understand the power of learning to love yourself and letting go of what others think. Similar to the lighthouse and sponge principle, when we speak or share our thoughts and talents with another our energy can either radiate out, or we can suck in the energy around us.

Let me explain.

Have you ever heard a speaker, preacher or someone who was passionate share a message? You may have been in the audience and literally felt the power of that message. Maybe the words pierced your heart, sinking deep into your soul, motivating you to action. You left feeling inspired and compelled to act, as though a flame was passed on from them to you.

That is the energy that someone who has a good self-image radiates. That is someone who is confident, who is using their God-given gifts and talents to better the world. They feel adequate and loved. Their energy spreads, filling the room and igniting an energy within those in attendance.

A great lighthouse was Martin Luther King, Jr. He had a way of speaking that reached the hearts of many people. It did not mean that he didn't struggle with feeling inadequate at times, he just didn't let it stop him. In fact, many people criticized his work and his message in the beginning. In 1966, a poll was taken that found that only about 33% of Americans had positive feelings about Dr. King. (Whitaker, 2013) Thank goodness he did not let what others thought of him prevent him from sharing his powerful, life changing directives on love and equality. He had a good self-image and knew he was able to radiate positive energy into the world.

On the other hand, if someone is feeling inadequate and has a poor self-image, just like the ugly rock they are always comparing themselves to others and worrying about what the people around them think. The energy they have is focused on themselves. People that come in contact with someone who has all the energy focused on themselves may notice that they feel tired and even drained of energy after being in their presence. Those with poor self-image cannot radiate their energy and message to the hearts of others because it is all spent on self-worry and doubt. They are letting the fear of what other's think of them stop them from using their God-given gifts and talents.

Quiz
Take this quiz to find out if you are letting what other's think of you stifle your potential. Rate each question on a scaled on 1-5 with 1 being very negative and 5 being super positive.

1. When you get ready in the morning you choose your outfit and look for the day based on what you want

to wear and the image you want to portray, NOT what you think others may want you to look like.

2. When you are in a crowd of people and have something to share, you feel confident in speaking up.
3. When you go to bed at night, you base the success of the day on how you felt, not on what other people said or might have thought about you.
4. You believe you have something important to offer the world.
5. You are calm and confident when meeting a new person.

If your score falls below 15, it is time for you to break free from those bonds of self-doubt. If you scored less than 20, keep stretching those wings, you can fly even higher.

You have a choice to feel adequate and to love yourself, or to let your negative self-image prevent you from fulfilling your potential and living a life that could benefit you and all of those around you. Step out of criticism, worry and doubt. Embrace love, confidence and potential. You have an individual blueprint within. You are the only one who has your particular gifts, experiences and passions – all of which create an important message and purpose unique to you. You were given those for a reason, you can help others and yourself find greater success and happiness as you choose to radiate that energy and message out to the world. But, you must begin with yourself. You must change the vision of who you are and what you can accomplish by learning to see the divine within.

You are divinely capable. You are loved. You are important. You are unique. You are more powerful than you think.

Embrace that power. Change the world and better lives, beginning with your own.

The following 3-day challenge I am going to share is very powerful. It will change your life if completed with diligence and exactness. Only move forward if you have a sincere desire to begin to change and see yourself through God's eyes.

Action Steps: Three Day Challenge

"Think success and it will happen."
-Thomas D. Willhite

Day 1

1. Before you get out of bed in the morning, smile and think, "This is the best day of my life!"
    - Before you do anything else take the time to meditate or pray. Express gratitude for the blessings in your life.
2. Imagine how you want your day to go.
    - How do you want to feel?
    - Who are you going to help?
    - What are you going to accomplish?
4. After your meditation or prayer, write down your intention for the day in your journal.
    - Pick one specific thing you would like to have happen that day. (For example, "Just for today I will speak calmly to my children.")

2. During the course of the day, reflect often on who you want to be and what you want to accomplish. This will be especially hard, but very helpful, when you find yourself in a less than desirable situation and you are put to the test.
3. Before you go to bed, take time to reflect on your day. This can be done through prayer or meditation.

"The unthankful heart... discovers no mercies; but let the thankful heart sweep through the day and, as the magnet finds the iron, so it will find, in every hour, some heavenly blessings!"
-Henry Ward Beecher

Day 2

1. Repeat all the steps for day one and...
2. Notice all the good things that happen to you throughout the day, however small they may be.
3. Before bed, record in your journal all of the good things that happened that day.

"You, yourself, as much as anybody in the entire universe, deserve your love and affection"
-Buddha

Day 3

1. Repeat all the steps for days one and two. Plus ...
2. Pray to be able to see yourself as God sees you. Then,...
3. Sit in front of a mirror for 10 minutes without thinking any critical thoughts or finding any flaws. You may only extend mental compliments and love to

yourself. Only positive thoughts are allowed. If you want a real challenge, every time you criticize yourself, start over!

4. Make a list of all the good things you accomplished during the day.

Part 4
Soul Intuition

When we are able to discover our God-given gifts, throwing off the layers of fear, helplessness and inadequacy that once covered their light, we will be able to embrace our own greatness and power to make a difference in the world.

~Allison Larsen

You have forgotten who you are... Look inside yourself...You are more than what you have become... Remember.

~The Lion King

10

Soul Action: The World's Way vs. God's Way

Dedicated to Natalie, who taught me God's way through her example.

There are two ways to go about living life in general. You can react to whatever is thrown your way. Or, you can decide who you are and who you want to become and you can act like it regardless of what life tosses at you.

In the previous chapter, we focused on shifting your perspective to be able to view challenges as opportunities for growth rather than trials. We learned that how we choose to think about a certain situation can either leave us feeling inadequate or loved.

Now, it is time to kick it up a notch and talk about soul action. Thoughts are important because they will lead to action. And, to really empower our soul, we must act instead of react. When we are able to shift our perspective and what we do matches our thought pattern, we have the ability to form habits that manifest what we have created in our mind.

If you are letting your behaviors, your situations in life and your reactions to them define you, then you are giving up your power to produce the life you want. You will go through life having never lived up to your full potential. If you choose to remember who you are and act as the divine being that you were created to be, no matter what life throws your way, you will be able to tap into your Soul Intuition and come out on top knowing you did your best and lived life to the fullest.

Many people get stuck in reaction mode. They feel as if they are victims to their circumstances and rather than act, they go throughout life reacting to situations. There is a specific pattern, called the reaction trap, that I see with people who are stuck feeling like victims. I use the word stuck very intentionally. People who view themselves as possible casualties to their circumstances are just trying to survive, to keep their heads above water. They are not proactive and they do not recognize potentially life-changing opportunities that are thrown their way. They react to their environment with certain emotions. They react to those emotions with certain behaviors. They let those behaviors define who they are and that affects their connection to the Divine Source. If you have been feeling stuck lately, you may be trapped in this pattern. Here are a couple of examples, see if you can relate.

Bill, a client of mine, worked at a high-end marketing firm. He was given a heavy work load and often found himself reacting to that heavy load by feeling stressed out. When Bill felt stressed out he would get angry and yell at his assistant. Momentarily, he admitted that he found some relief by yelling at her because she would realize how stressed he was and he wouldn't feel alone. However, after only a few minutes Bill would regret lashing out and he would experience guilt. He would think about what a "bad boss" and a "mean person" he was. He would feel frazzled and low on energy for the rest of the day. He described feeling that his higher power, the universe, was not pleased with his actions. Here was Bill's reaction trap:

Environment: Heavy workload
Emotion: Anger
Behavior: Yelling at his assistant
Payoff: Momentary relief
Negative labels placed on self: Bad boss and mean person
Connection to Higher Power: Felt the universe was not pleased with his actions

Bill let his emotions and then his behaviors define who he was, putting a negative label on himself that affected his performance. Sound familiar? You may not work at a high end marketing firm, but I bet you have found yourself in the same reaction mode as Bill.

I work with many parents who struggle with the reaction trap. Amber, a client of mine, was a mother of three small children. Her kids would make huge messes all over the house throughout the day. Amber would feel very frustrated because it seemed like she could spend all day picking up after them and the house would never be clean! Sometimes she would get so fed up that she would spank her children. In the moment she said that she found a small amount of relief because she was able to express her frustration and punish her children for causing her so much stress. However, shortly thereafter Amber felt horrible and thoughts like, "I am the worst mom" or "I am such a bully" would enter her mind. She would feel discouraged and after the spanking episodes would often call her husband in tears begging him to come home early from work. Amber felt that God was displeased with her.

Environment: Messy house
Emotion: Frustrated
Behavior: Spanking kids
Payoff: Momentary relief
Negative labels placed on self: Bad mom and bully
Connection to Higher Power: God was displeased with her

Amber let her emotions and her behaviors define who she was, putting a negative label on herself that affected her ability to parent.

These are just two examples out of thousands of clients that I have worked with that are literally stuck in the reaction trap. It is a trap that many people don't even realize that they are caught in. It is a vicious cycle that will continue until they recognize what is going on and learn how to act from their Soul Intuition instead of react.

So, how do you take soul action, really become empowered to create the life you want? You have to change the pattern.

Notice how in both of the examples my clients found themselves reacting to their environment with an emotion. They reacted to the emotion they felt with a certain behavior. They reacted to their poor behavior by labeling themselves with a negative term. Finally, the reaction to the negative label was lower energy and discouragement caused by the feeling that they were disconnected from their higher power. Their souls felt stuck.

Has this ever happened to you? What can you do to get unstuck?

Enter Soul Action. Soul Action is the opposite of the reaction trap.

Let's take Bill. The first thing I asked him after realizing he was stuck in a negative pattern was what his "Capital T Truth" was about his relationship with his higher power. He reported that he felt that the universe was set up to give everyone abundance and that he had a valuable place in it. I then asked him what label he would put on himself that would act in accordance to his belief. He said that he would call himself a powerful being of light. The payoff for knowing that was that he felt capable and full of potential. I questioned him on how he wanted to act when he remembered who he was. He reported that he wanted his behavior to be uplifting and positive to those around him, increasing the frequency in the universe. When I inquired as to what emotions he was feeling after thinking about his place in the universe and who he was, he reported that he felt calm, confident and centered.

He was ready to act in accordance to who he was and who he wanted to become. I challenged him to use the Soul Action pattern next time he felt overloaded at work. Sure enough, Bill reported feeling much more productive, happy and connected when he implemented what he had learned and chose to act instead of react. Let's take a look at Bill's Soul Action pattern:

Connection to Higher Power: Abundant and valuable
Label: Powerful being of light
Payoff: Capable and full of potential
Behavior: Uplifting and positive
Emotions: Calm, confident and centered

Environment: Productively busy

Amber had a similar experience when she remembered how God felt about her and acted accordingly. She was able to choose how she wanted to act based on her beliefs rather than feeling guilty for reacting to her emotions.

Do you let your emotions control you or are you in control of your life?

The world's way is the reaction trap. It is have-do-be. You have a problem, so you do something in reaction and that action defines who you be-come. God's way is Soul Action, it is be-do-have. You remember who you want to be-come and you choose what to do accordingly. As a result, you have the ability to create the life you want.

The first thing to be aware of when using soul action is your connection to your higher power. From whom or where do you feel like you get your divine truth and light? Tapping into something greater than just your mortal emotions will help you see a bigger picture.

Once you recognize your higher power, you have identified your power source, the origin of never ending light, energy and love. If you can learn how to access that when you are feeling down or unmotivated, you will have the incentive and inspiration to be your very best self.

The next step is to identify your soul potential, who you are deep down, your ideal self, as well as who you feel like you have the potential to become. If you get really clear on this, you will know exactly how you need to act to reach your full potential. Here are some questions to help you get really specific.

Quiz
Get a pen and a paper and take a moment to jot down a few words in response to each question.

1. What does God, or your higher power, believe you are capable of?
2. If you could paint a picture of your ideal self, what would that look like?
3. At the end of your life, what do you want people to say about you?
4. When do you feel the most fulfilled, like you are making a difference in the world?
5. Who do you admire and why? What traits of theirs would you like to emulate?

You must decide who you are and who you want to become if you want to stop reacting and begin taking action, regaining control of your life and where you want to go. Once you have determined who you want to be, then you can act like you are already there. Pretty soon those actions will turn into habits and before you know it you will be living up to your soul's potential. Answering these questions will help you get started. Use your Soul Intuition and look within to really discover who you are capable of being.

Stop living below your potential. Stop letting your circumstances define you. Figure out what you want and take action to get it. It can be done. I have helped thousands of people do it. I have done it myself. I am not promising or even hinting that it will be easy, but it will be so worth it.

Just like I mentioned in a previous chapter, once we take control of our life, recognizing that we can create what we want, we also have to accept responsibility for the things that do not go right, that do not work in our favor. It is more difficult to feel responsible for your failures, but it is so worth it to own your mistakes so that you can embrace your potential and fulfill your divine destiny!

After you have determined who you are and who you want to become, then you can determine what behavior manifests your ideal self. You can choose exactly how you want to behave in any situation. You now have a standard, something at least for which you can strive. The thing about behavior is that every human action has a conscious or subconscious payoff.

"Even the most destructive behaviors have a payoff. If you did not perceive the behavior in question to generate some value to you, you would not do it."
~Dr. Phil

He is right! Did you notice in my above examples that both Bill and Amber experienced momentary relief or satisfaction immediately after they reacted poorly to their situation? The guilt and self-criticism they experienced afterwards was not worth the brief payoff, but it was there. If we are going to act instead of react, we must perceive that there is a payoff. That reward comes as we realize what we are trying to accomplish and who we are striving to become. When our actions are in alignment with our goals and potential, we will experience an extreme sense of satisfaction and physical success in all areas of our lives.

When you encounter a problem, simply remember who you are and behave accordingly. Act instead of react.

> When you encounter a problem, remember who you are and act accordingly.
>
> soulintuition.com

Once you have determined how you want to behave and act accordingly, you will find that those negative emotions that used to control your behaviors have turned into positive and empowering emotions. Common emotions clients that use the Soul Actions pattern report feel are:

- Confident
- Calm
- Collected
- In-Control
- Peaceful

The last component of the pattern is the environment. In Bill's case, his was a stressful workplace. Amber's was a messy house. In each situation, after working with these clients to change, Bill's job and Amber's kids were still there. But thankfully, the way that they perceived things was different. The work environment went from "stressful" to "productively busy." The "messy" house became a "training ground" for responsible children. Thus, going from a reaction trap to Soul Action. Here is a chart that you can use to help yourself walk through problems God's way instead of the world's way.

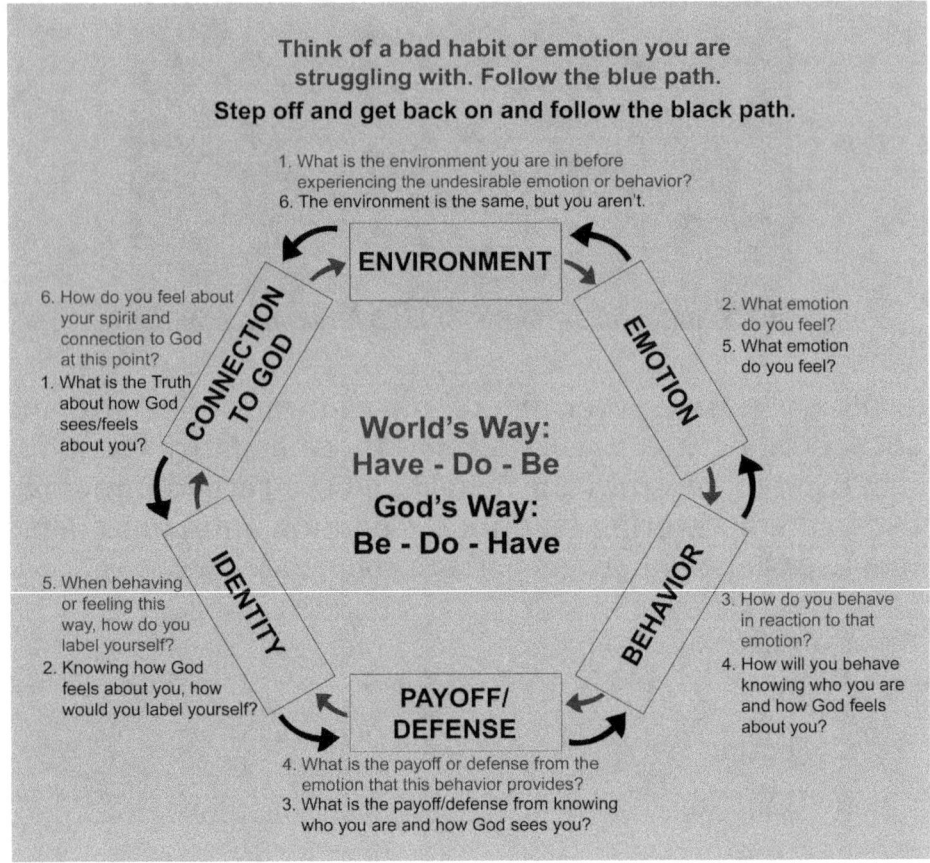

I have seen this exercise change lives. If you are ready to change yours, to begin to shift your behaviors and emotions to the positive, use this exercise to begin living more fully to your potential.

Action Steps

1. Write down a list of things of you are struggling with.
2. Use the patterns walk to work through each struggle using the chart provided.

3. Recognize and start to implement God's way rather than the world's way. You will be able to tap into your Soul Intuition and take Soul Action to create the life you want!

"Play to your strengths."

"I haven't got any," said Harry, before he could stop himself.

"Excuse me," growled Moody, *"you've got strengths if I say you've got them. Think now. What are you best at?"*

~J.K. Rowling, Harry Potter and the Goblet of Fire

11

Soul Weakness: Finding Gifts

Dedicated to all my past mentors and coaches who helped me discover my greatest strengths and weaknesses.

Do you feel like Harry? Do you ever wonder what your strengths are or question if you even have any?

I often hear people admit they are slow to recognize their God-given gifts and talents. When my clients ask, I give them one powerful, surprising piece of advice.

If you want to find your strengths, the first place to look is behind your weaknesses.

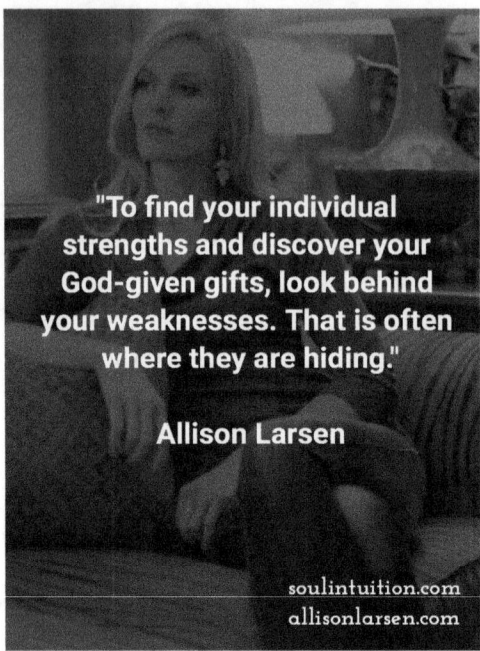

Now, you may be thinking that this is counterintuitive, and on the surface it is. But, when you use your Soul Intuition and dive deep down and connect with your soul, you will find your hidden strengths waiting to be discovered behind your faults. A wonderful mentor of mine first brought this to my attention years ago. She told me that our weaknesses are just strengths turned up too high. As I pondered this statement, my soul recognized Truth. I began to look at myself.

People have told me that one of my weaknesses is that I am a pleaser. But, when I look close I recognize that my strength is caring about others. My compassion enables me to truly help people. Another weakness is that I get obsessed with things and even was diagnosed with OCD as young teenager. The strength behind this is that I have an amazing ability to focus. This gift has served me well over the years, allowing me to be fully present and give my best self when working with clients, writing a book, playing with my kids, etc. I just had to learn to direct my focus to serve me, rather than hinder me.

Are you getting the idea? What makes us different, what sets us apart, those things that we may think are broken about ourselves can actually be the greatest gifts we have to offer the world. We just need to learn how to use them. There are many examples of leaders and innovators who were considered flawed before they became great. What made these people so great, and ultimately the key to their success and ability to powerfully influence and change the world, was their capacity to ignore their labels and embrace their peculiarities. They learned to turn them into vehicles to accomplish things. Here are just a few examples:

Albert Einstein

As a young child, Albert Einstein was considered wild and struggled at school. He often felt alienated and unaccepted. Eventually, he dropped out and later found a way to dodge the draft in Germany. It became apparent that Albert did not thrive in highly conformist and structured environments. However, rather than consider himself dumb and inadequate, he recognized that he had amazing talents in physics and math and found a way to get an education in Switzerland, a more liberal setting where he thrived and made many good friends. After graduation, things did not always come easily for Einstein. He struggled to find a steady position and was turned down by many potential employers because of his independent thinking and lack of conformity. Again, he refused to let this perceived weakness define him. Eventually, Einstein used his ability to think radically and outside the box to discover concepts, such as the Theory of Relativity and E=mc^2, that would change the world forever. The very things many considered to be weaknesses were the driving factor behind some of history's greatest successes.

Oprah Winfrey

Oprah's first boss told her that she was not right for television because she was too emotional. She could have listened to him and quit but instead, she decided to embrace her gift to connect with people. This once perceived weakness became Winfrey's greatest strength as she grew to be the highest paid television star and one of the world's most loved celebrities. Oprah is celebrated for her ability to move her audiences by tapping into their emotions. The very thing that her first boss once saw as a weakness, Oprah was able to embrace and use as her greatest strength.

Walt Disney

Walt Disney was often thought of as an unrealistic dreamer who lived with his head in clouds. He was told many times throughout his life that his ideas would never be a success. Despite constant criticism, financial struggle, hardships and even abuse, Walt refused to look at himself as a failure. Sure, he experienced failures in certain areas of his life, but he did not give in to the idea that he was different and thus could not become successful. We all know how his story ended. The unrealistic dreamer helped many people make their dreams come true despite the financial, mental and emotional traumas he experienced as a young child.

Traumatic experiences such as abuse can be a huge block when we are trying to discover our gifts if we don't address past issues. Many people even view those experiences as weaknesses, things that they want to hide. But, the strength that can come from taking the time to heal is powerful. Some of the strongest people I know are survivors of trauma and/or abuse.

Trauma is caused by something out of our control yet it can control our lives. Abuse is one of the worst traumas a person can endure. Ghosts from the past can haunt a victim for years, tormenting their soul, and preventing them from being able to fully invest in themselves and embrace their talents and gifts. It affects their energy and can sabotage a person's potential to find success. Regardless of good intentions or positive plans, a person will never be able to completely invest energetically in themselves until they have taken the necessary steps to fully heal from an abusive past.

It is easy to bottle up old ghosts and then hide them in the very deepest crevices of our souls, but they are still there. Sometimes, when least expected they will escape. As painful as it is to face those phantoms, I have never met an abuse victim that has regretted taking the time to endure short-term suffering for long-term success. There are simple steps that anyone can take to begin. I call them the 4 R's of healing.

Recognize: Take time to recognize the negative emotions when they come. Write them down on a piece of paper. Putting a specific label on an emotion will allow you to identify what you are truly feeling.

Release: Once you have taken the time to write down your negative emotions, burn the paper. Find a safe place and set it on fire with the intention that you are also letting go of those feelings that have weighed you down for so long.

Replace: Now you have an empty space to fill within your soul. On a fresh piece of paper write down how you want to feel using descriptive words such as happy, peaceful, and confident. Hang it somewhere where you will see it often.

Repeat: Be patient with yourself walking through these steps as often as necessary.

This process works. It involves the subconscious and conscious mind. You will find that, over time, the ghosts disappear and you are able to invest fully in yourself and discovering your God-given gifts.

Another common obstacle that gets in the way of recognizing and embracing our potential is comparison. We are each unique and have varying individual talents. Often people will compare the things they are not good at with someone else's natural talents.

For example, I was mentoring a client of mine the other day. She told me how she could never be successful at her own network marketing business because she was not as outgoing as her husband. He was very talented at speaking and engaging large groups of people. She was not comfortable in front of a crowd and found that she could not communicate clearly.

Instead of focusing on her husband's talents, I shifted the conversation and began asking her questions about what she felt like her talents were. She reported that she had a very strong ability to connect with others in a personal setting. She reported that often people were moved to action after an intimate discussion with her. I helped her to tap into her Soul Intuition to be able to identify this as a major strength. We then discussed how this God-given gift to connect personally could be used as a powerful tool to grow her business.

Are you comparing yourself to someone? If so, stop spending energy focusing on someone else's gifts and start looking at your own. You can use all that extra energy to discover ways that you can use your unique talents to bless your own life and make the world a better place.

Each of us is born with specific gifts and those gifts, in combination with the experiences we have in life, give us an individual skill set that we can offer the world. No one else has your combination of talents, personality and background.

There is only one you in the world. What will you do with the gifts you have been given?

Recently, I was speaking with a friend and client who lives in California. She has worked in television for the past 5 years. This woman is beautiful, dynamic and great on camera. She has interviewed celebrities and other notable personalities and has a real talent for it. As we spoke she told me that her true desire and goal in life is to help people but, because of past experiences, recognized that she did not do well working one on one. She felt much more comfortable sharing her message of self-help in a setting with large groups of people where she did not have to interact with them on an individual basis.

This beautiful, talented friend of mine told me that she had a powerful message to share with the world that she is passionate about. Despite a natural affinity for the medium, she said, "I really want to help people, a lot of people, but I can't do that through TV."

Early in her life she experienced a combination of occurrences and conversations that led her to internalize the message that being on camera was shallow and vain. She believed that in order to make a difference, she had to work with individuals in a personal setting, caring for them one by one. She felt she had to give up her talent for television in order to make a difference in people's lives.

As I had her write down her list of talents, passions and desires for life, she began to recognize that reaching the masses through television was part of her divine blueprint for happiness. As we continued to discuss her desire to help others, she finally realized what a powerful gift her television presence could be. Rather than an outlet for meaningless drivel, she could use television to deliver a powerful message to the masses. She just needed to let go of her false beliefs.

False beliefs, likes those my client had embraced for most of her life can be a major hurdle preventing you from recognizing your God-given gifts and reaching your full potential. False beliefs are limiting. Maybe as a young child, you were told like my client above that there was something that you couldn't do and you are still hanging on to that. Some common false beliefs that my clients struggle with are surrounding limits because of their gender, education level or culture.

What are your false beliefs and how are they limiting you?

I once worked with a powerful mentor who taught me a great deal about being successful. He owns a thriving business, helps people all over the world, and is affluent. Interestingly, he did not do well in school and never graduated from college. Many people told him that he would never be successful without a college education, so for years he believed it. One day he was introduced to a mentor that taught him to let go of that limiting belief and embrace his gifts. He did and never looked back. I am so thankful that he shed the bonds that limited him because I have benefited greatly from his unique talents as well as hundreds of thousands of other people all over the world.

Let go of the beliefs that are limiting you. You are a divine being capable of great things.

If you can embrace your God-given gifts and let go of preconceived notions about what you can and cannot do, you will fly. Don't let anything hold you back. You are meant for greatness. You have the power within you to change the world in a way that only you can. It is your choice. Do you want to be limited or limitless?

The last component of learning to find your strengths I am going to address in this chapter is learning to honor your inner child. Often times we view that little voice inside of us telling us what she needs as a weakness, but if we learn to listen we can find our gifts and align with our purpose. What do I mean?

I want you to think of a toddler you know. We are going to dive into the 2-year old psyche. What would happen if you ignored this toddler for a long period of time? Or, what might happen if that small child really wanted something, but didn't get it? One word comes to mind: Tantrum! Why throw a fit? Because a tantrum demands attention. It is almost impossible to ignore a screaming two-year old. All you parents know what I mean!

Now, think of a picture of yourself when you were younger. You were probably cute, and if you are anywhere close to my age, you might be wearing a yarn bow in your hair or an old-school Lacoste sweater with a pair of plaid pants. It was so long ago, you might not even recognize yourself. Perhaps you feel disconnected from this little being and can't believe that was you at one time in your life.

Well, believe it or not, that little being is still a part of you. When I was younger, I used to stomp my foot if things didn't go my way. To this day, I feel like a good stomp when I don't get what I want.

So now that we have brushed up on our child psychology and reconnected with our past, what does all this have to do with finding our strengths?

That younger version of yourself lives within you. Often times in yoga, we refer to that part of our self as our inner child. Just like a two-year old, our inner child throws a fit when we ignore her, or she is not getting what she wants. What does that tantrum look like? It can be illness, depression, anxiety or a number of other unpleasantries that we label as weaknesses. Just like a toddler throwing a fit, these "tantrums" serve a purpose. They are impossible to ignore and force us to start paying attention to ourselves. So, how do we avoid these "fits"?

Listen.

Learn to listen to your inner child. If you give her the attention she needs, she will not throw tantrums. You will find that you get ill less often and that you are more content and happy with your life. Not only that, you will find that as you listen to what your body needs, you will be able to take better care of yourself and may even discover some amazing new gifts along the way.

How do we listen to this little girl or boy that lives inside us? I like to think of that picture of when I was younger and imagine having a conversation with that little girl. "Allison," I say, "how are you doing?" If I tune in, she will let me know. So often as adults, we get stuck in the trap of pretending everything is okay even when it is not. The thing I admire about toddlers and young children is their honesty, and my inner child is always honest with me.

Psalms 8:2 says, "Out of the mouth of babes has thou ordained strength..." You will find that your gifts are strengthened as you learn to listen to that inner child.

Use your God-given gifts to do something you feel passionate about. This will lead you to really make a difference in the world in a way that is as unique to you as your gifts. You will be able to go to bed each night feeling fulfilled and successful.

Don't let the world define you.
Don't let past experiences and conversations limit you.
Embrace the qualities that set you apart.
Look within to find answers. Your strengths are there. They may just be hiding behind negative labels of perceived weaknesses.

Action Steps

1. Write down a list of things that you feel are your weaknesses.

2. Across from each, list one potential strength that could be hiding behind it.

For example:
Too trusting - The ability to love and see good in other people
Obsessed - Strong focus
Too emotional - Can connect with people on a deep level

As you do this, you will find your gifts and let go of your weaknesses.

However else you live your life, live it freely. It is not the years in your life that count, it is the life in your years.

~Adlai Stevenson

12

Soul Intuition Implemented

Dedicated to you, because you made it.

If you have read to this point in the book, congratulations! You have learned the skills necessary to help you let go of fear, helplessness and inadequacy. You have learned how to embrace success, empowerment and love. You are tapping into your Soul Intuition and discovering your God-given gifts.

Following are powerful tips that you can use to further develop your Soul Intuition.

Tip #1: Find your message.

You were born with a unique blueprint for greatness. You were given divine gifts and talents. You have had opportunities and experiences that helped to shape you and make you who you are today.

There is only one you.

You have been blessed with gifts and experiences that can be shared with others to help make the world a better place.

For years I struggled to find my message. I didn't really feel like I was particularly gifted or that I had any miraculous survival tales or a rags to riches story. But, then I began to tap into my Soul Intuition. As I did many of the things that I suggested to you in this book, I started to recognize that I had a unique message. I discovered my God-given gifts and reflected on the lessons I had been taught throughout my life. Because I took the time and effort to recognize the greatness within myself, I am now able to help people all over the world better about their lives. My life is better. I feel fulfilled. I feel happy. I feel successful. At the end of the day I can reflect back and know that in some way I made the world a better place.

To find your message, make a list of things about which you are passionate and a list of your talents. You will find that there may be similar things on both lists. There is your first clue. Now, write down 3 experiences that you feel shaped your life and under each write one thing that you learned. Last, combine the similar words and the lessons learned. That is your message. It may not be polished yet, but it is there. Trust me.

In order to spread the message you have found within, use the tools you have learned in the book to get over your fears when it comes to sharing your gifts and message with the world. It can be scary. Trust me, I know. On a regular basis I am doing new things to help myself grow and to spread my light to the world. It is uncomfortable, it is hard and sometimes I still experience fear, but I do it anyway. Why? Because I have learned how and because I have learned that it is so worth it.

Using your unique gifts and talents to share your individual message to the world will give you a sense of purpose. You will discover your unique place in the universe as you uncover your talents and overcome the fear of sharing them. Deep down, it is that need to belong and feel like you are making a difference that is at the root of most people's ability to feel happy and successful in life. Finding your message and sharing it from your heart will help you find greater success and happiness.

Be brave and be powerful. As you overcome your fears and your feelings of inadequacy you will be able to deliver your life-changing message.

There is a power unparalleled when one learns to speak from the heart and share the things they are passionate about in an uninhibited form. The message being delivered is freed from the cage of self-doubt and is allowed to take flight into the hearts and souls of listeners. Lives will be altered, spiritual gifts opened and divine messages financed with the wealth of courage and confidence that accompanies the messages of those who speak unrestrained by bonds of self-consciousness and self-doubt.

> There is a power unparalleled when one learns to speak from the heart and share the things they are passionate about in an uninhibited form. The message being delivered is freed from the cage of self-doubt and is allowed to take flight into the hearts and souls of listeners.
>
> Lives will be altered, spiritual gifts opened and divine messages financed with the wealth of courage and confidence that accompanies the messages of those who speak unrestrained by bonds of self-consciousness and self-doubt.
>
> soulintuition.com
> allisonlarsen.com

Tip #2: Find your why

Why do you want to discover your God-given gifts? Why do you want to live to your fullest potential?

For every success in life there is a cost. It would be easier just to sit at home, hidden from the world watching television and eating chips all day. You wouldn't have as many failures. You wouldn't have to deal with as much emotion. You wouldn't have to worry about what other people thought, or if you were doing the right things. But yet, here you are, taking the time to read this book, to invest in yourself. You must want to make a difference in the world. Why?

Why do you feel the desire to make a difference? Is it for you? Is it for your family? Is it for God?

It is crucial that you determine your *why* and write it down, because there will be costs to pay along the way and you will have to decide if it is worth it. If you have a powerful *why* and you remember it, all the challenges and struggles will pay off. At the end of the day, you will be able to look yourself in the eye and feel like you made a difference.

Many people get hung up on the *how*. They spend all of their energy focusing on how they are going to be successful or reach a certain goal. What I have discovered in my experience is that the *how* is really not very important. I will let you in on a secret that has brought me and my clients great success. Focus on the *why*.

First find your *why* and become very clear on it. I often suggest a writing exercise to the people I work with that involves taking the time to write down their *why* for what they want to accomplish in life. I direct them to use a lot of emotion packed words that describe the passions and beliefs that drive their *why*. This exercise does not include any specifics like job titles, amount of money or time frames. I then have my clients come up with some power packed "I am" statements that I call affirmations based on their *why*. Here are some examples:

"I am an instrument in the Lord's hands in sharing my message."

"I am a loving mother and wife who lifts and supports her family."

"I am a powerful speaker who inspires his audience to action."

If you say affirmations out loud daily to help remind you of your *why*, you will start consciously and subconsciously making decisions that will attract those things into your life.

It isn't all that hard or time consuming to figure out your *why*. In fact, I bet your soul will give a sigh of relief when you take a moment to finally look within and acknowledge it. Know that you are empowered with the ability to find your *why* and change your life, it is as simple as just deciding to do it.

"One day you finally knew what you had to do, and began..."

~Mary Oliver

Tip #3: Use Your Soul Intuition

This may seem a bit redundant, but just because you have done all the things I spoke about in this book one time, it doesn't mean that you are good to go for the rest of your life. To reach your full potential, you must keep going. Review these steps. Re-read this book as often as you want, each time making sure to implement something new. There are important things that you will do now, as well as years down the road. Don't lose focus. Remember what you have learned and implement it. It will change your life.

In the end, the choice is yours. Will you choose to use the things you have learned to tap into your Soul Intuition, discovering your God-given gifts and fulfilling your divine potential? When we look within, we are empowered to define ourselves and create the life we want.

You have learned to let go of fear, helplessness and inadequacy and are ready to invite success, empowerment and love into your life. You know how to use your Soul Intuition. You know how to recognize your God-given gifts. You know how to live the life you were designed to live. Are you ready to begin? Are you ready to use your talents to help yourself and to make the world around you a better place?

Soul Intuition Success Stories

Throughout the book I have shared stories from my clients and mentors to illustrate the concepts and practices of Soul Intuition from their own perspective and in their own words. I have asked them to share how Soul Intuition has impacted their lives and helped them to let go of fear, helplessness and inadequacy and led them to embrace success, empowerment and love. I hope you find inspiration here as you progress towards finding your own message, your why and your Soul Intuition.

Soul Perspective
Bethany Teeple is an Organizational Mentor I have known for a year. She first came to me to work on her perceptions of wellness. Together we discussed how to turn her have-to's into wants. Today, she is using her God-given gifts to speak and inspire people all over the country, as well as through mentoring groups.

My earliest memories as a young child included a desire to be a mom. Then I got married! I could not wait to have children. Three kids later I realized how much work it was to be a parent. However, I still knew that I wanted to have more children. So the next three bundles of joy came to our home. I continued to embrace being a mother, however, doubts started to pop up in my mind of whether I was good enough. These doubts began to take over my motherhood, but I want to share how I have shifted my doubts to become my strengths. Learning how to control my thoughts and my words are key to this process working. I shifted my thoughts to "I get to be their mom. I get to learn from them. They are my greatest teachers."

We had lived in our new home for about a year when we had our 6th child. It was a big house to manage but located in a wonderful neighborhood full of amazingly talented women. While that sounds ideal, I began to have many feelings of inadequacy. I started to think that I had to be just like everyone else. I began comparing other's amazingness to my faults. I started to let myself feel like a victim in my life. I would think "I have to do the laundry. I have to clean the house. I have to make all the dinners. I have to drive the kids to all their activities. I have to clean up after everyone. I have to exercise. I have to lose weight. I have to.... And the list goes on and on." Let me tell you, that is a lot of pressure. Those intense feelings of "have to" along with feelings of "I am never going to be enough."

Let me share with you an analogy of a pressure cooker. If well managed, the pressure of a pressure cooker can help you can vegetables and meats. It is a very useful item to have in your home to preserve your food. However, the same pressure cooker has the ability to cause a great amount of harm. If you allow the pressure to get too high it can explode, hurting you and making a huge mess. I remember as a child when my mother was canning food she was very attentive to the pressure gauge. If the pressure in life gets too high, it will hurt us, but as we learn to manage the pressure in our life we can experience great levels of joy in our life.

How did I overcome these thoughts and feelings? Honestly, I still need to work on it at times. However, I began to realize that God sent these beautiful children to me because I was the perfect person to be their mom. Notice I did not say the perfect mom, just the person that needed to teach my children and my children to teach me. I began to recognize what a privilege I had to be a mom. I began to feel gratitude and it started to change my perception of the things that I thought I had to do.

Learning to let go has impacted my life beyond measure. Actually over the process of a couple of years, I learned what things in my life were making me feel overwhelmed. I observed that the "things" in my home and even my home itself impacted my feelings. I realized that I had too much home for me to manage. So after a lot of prayer, my husband and I decided to move to a small town and buy a smaller home. We simplified. I let go! Wow!

My life changed as I have learned to let go of "things" and turn to God for the source of my joy. Instead of my things, how I looked and what others thought of me, I now had a greater source of joy. I still get overwhelmed, feel inadequate and not good enough sometimes. However, the difference is that I know how to overcome it. I know how to change my thoughts which then impact my actions. Our thoughts are so powerful. They can influence for good or bad. The faster that we can see our negative thoughts the faster we can change them.

Learn more about Bethany on GloriousReflections.com.

Soul Healing

I first met Alex Speiser 4 years ago when he was serving a religious mission in my town and struggling with physical illness. Together we worked on empowering Alex to change his mindset and take control of his own health. Today Alex is helping people do the same through foot zoning, classes and personal coaching sessions.

I remember when Allison first introduced me to this idea of being conscious of my true identity and separating it from my illness. I had never considered just how powerful an effect I was having upon myself by identifying myself as a "sick" person.

I obtained Allison's help when I was going through the worst physical health of my life. It seemed that my days were as unpredictable as the weather. One moment I would be fine, the next I would find myself with a fever, fatigue and sharp stabbing pains hurting my digestive system. When this came on I would have to lie down and rest until the symptoms passed. What was worse, I had spent the previous year battling deadly illnesses I got from spending time in a third-world country. So, by the time I met Allison I was deep in not just physical, but emotional distress. I told myself every day and to many people I knew that, "I am sick all the time," or, "I'm always sick."

I really could not see any future for me as a healthy person. All I could envision was a version of myself that was pathetic, always needing help to recover from frequent spells and never able to do much. But I had determined that despite this being who I was, I would strive to be cheerful and soldier on. As noble as such an idea may have appeared, it was honestly draining and underlined with misery that I assumed was just a part of my life.

Once I separated my illness and symptoms from my identity I experienced something extraordinary—my health improved dramatically both physically and emotionally. I not only became free from my physical symptoms, I experienced a transformation in my emotional maturity and mental capacity that enabled me to start helping others on a large scale. The power of aligning my identity with my true self and potential rather than my physical circumstances was the key to unlocking my personal power to achieve.

This principle is not only applicable to physical illness but is equally applicable to the emotional illnesses we all have regarding our dreams, potential, relationships, money, etc. I have used this principle to improve my life in all areas to enjoy freedom, and now I work as a professional freedom expert to teach others how to excel in all the most fundamental areas of their lives to enjoy true fulfillment. This principle is fundamental to everything I teach audiences and in seminars and to clients in one-on-one sessions."

You can follow Alex on facebook.com/nexusmentoring or alexunlimited.wordpress.com.

Soul Empowerment

I first met Cheryl Cox at a class of mine that she attended. She was immediately drawn to the principles that were taught and was very quick to embrace them and apply them into her life. I have watched her blossom into a confident foot zone practitioner and a leader who inspires many people in her area to let go of their blocks and move towards their goals at an accelerated pace.

The moment I heard the question, "Do you want to be a lighthouse or a sponge?" it immediately resonated with me. My initial worry was about work; I feared I was taking on the sorrows and pain of my clients. I was afraid I would not be able to continue my practice as a Foot Zone Reflexology therapist, the job I so passionately loved! I felt that I had to take on my clients' pain in order to empathize with them. I would go through waves of nausea, headaches and complete exhaustion during or after a session. I would have bouts of anger and sadness after working with clients that had released resentment issues or grief. I knew I had to do something or my work would not be able to continue. I expressed my concern to my dear mentor Allison and that is when she asked me the question:

"Do you want to be a lighthouse or a sponge?"

It really hit me in a profound way. I would much rather be a lighthouse, I LOVE lighthouses!

As I worked to learn how to better shield myself from the energy I was absorbing like a sponge, I realized that I may be doing this in other areas of my life. I started analyzing ALL my relationships and started noticing how much negativity I was taking on. When my husband came home stressed from work, I would get stressed out. Same with my children, if they were sad or frustrated, so was I. I even noticed when they got sick, within an hour I was having the same symptoms they were even though it is impossible to catch something from them that quickly. I really felt like an icky sponge!

The awareness alone helped me immensely, I wanted to radiate my light every day and show others the way! I made changes in my daily rituals to help shield me from negative energy. I'm so happy and grateful that I am able to continue to work with the same passion and, although not perfect, I am able to catch myself now and work every day towards being the lighthouse I want to be. Thank you Allison!

Cheryl offers workshops and information at www.HealthyandWellAllWays.com.

Soul Thoughts
I first met Amber Peterson when our girls became friends in the first grade. They are now about to enter their senior year of high school! She is the one who introduced me to foot zoning and energy work. Without her inspired guidance and encouragement I would not be where I am today.

I had just delivered my fourth child and was in mommy bliss! Holding this pure and precious spirit in my arms was heavenly. My husband, children and mother had visited us in the hospital for a couple hours and then headed home to get a good night's rest. A couple hours after their visit, I began to feel light headed, like something was wrong, but didn't know what. I was awake and aware of my surroundings, but for some reason I was frozen. Eventually, the nurse came in to help me out of bed when she realized I was hemorrhaging and blood was pooling inside of me. What happened afterwards was a traumatic experience for me. A life changing experience that took me to excruciating pain that night and for years to come. My whole body ached and back pain became the new normal for me.

Over time I found myself hiding in silence with depression. I began to doubt my contribution to my family and to the world. I became critical of myself and those around me.

This was not the real me and I kept asking myself what was wrong with me? I spent thousands of dollars going from doctor to doctor, year after year. One morning I asked myself, "If I feel this terrible at 30, how am I going to feel at age 40, 50, 60, and so on?" I didn't like the mental image of my future self and it scared me. I decided I needed to take my health in my own hands.

I began to ask holistic practitioners questions about how the body works. I began to read books about the body and healthy eating. One particular book taught about how thoughts create healing and that we can choose to live happy, healthy lives. It was the principles in that book that set my journey in motion for true healing. I let go of the old script of sickness and pain and replaced it with affirmations of being healed and whole. I learned about the anatomy of my spirit and how it functions with the physical body. I started to visualize rivers of God's light flowing through my body and healing me. Because I chose to let the darkness go I was able to feel more of His Love, which helped me heal at a deeper level.

Over time, I began to change as a person. I became more happy, more vibrant and healthy. I became stronger, more loving and more genuine than the person I was before the traumatic experience. I look back at the experience in the hospital as a life defining moment. It set me on a course that could either make me or break me. I chose to see it as a gift to transform me.

I feel empowered to know that when my body expresses itself in pain, it is my soul trying to get my attention. It is my soul sending me a message that I need to look at the core emotion that is causing the physical pain. Why not use this as an opportunity to realize that our bodies serve as a great tool to help us realign ourselves with our creator?

When faced with a trial or challenge, I now look inward and upward. For instance, if I am feeling pain, I express gratitude for the experience to help me come to an awareness to the hidden emotion. Gratitude may be the last thing on my mind with intense pain, but when I push through it by expressing gratitude to an all knowing creator and ask what I need to learn it opens my soul to higher understanding. I now know that if my stomach is hurting, I may be anxious or insecure about myself, another person or a situation. Instead of going to medication or dulling the discomfort with food or other forms of self-medication, I have an innate discipline that helps me tap into greater light and knowledge.

How grateful I am for learning how thoughts create healing! It's truth that sets us free from the darkness that we experience. May eternal truths be in your thought process, your belief system and resonate on a physical level so that you can live the life you were meant to live!"

Learn more about Amber at heartmindsuccess.com or contact her at peacewithoils@gmail.com.

Soul Love
Annette and I have known each other since college. We have both been on amazing life journeys since then. Annette now uses her God-given gifts and talents in the healing arts to help nurture people so they can recognize and embrace their true nature and step into their own power. She has helped many find greater happiness and joy, including me!

Learning to see myself through God's eyes has changed my life for the better. I never really had a problem with my self image until I was around 27 years old. Up until that time, I pretty much always knew I was beautiful. I had grown up the youngest child and the only girl. I was doted on and even had the nickname "Miss America." I was pretty and I knew it. I was always skinny and then after puberty, I had a nice body... I was thinly framed but also had curves. I was never lacking attention from the opposite sex. My first boyfriend was at the age of 11, and I don't ever remember not having one from that time until I married at the age of 21.

After I married, I started having children right away. I had three children in six years. After I had my first and second baby, my stomach was almost immediately flat again. Then, within a few months, I'd be back to about 120 pounds and in my size four clothes. I was right on track to do the same thing after I had my third baby. When he was one month old, I had lost almost all the weight I had gained and was feeling pretty good about how I looked. Then, I found out something that shocked me and hurt my feelings so badly my body went into a fight or flight response. As a result, my cortisol levels went through the roof. Even though I was eating healthy and working out regularly at a gym, I gained THIRTY POUNDS IN THIRTY DAYS! Just from stress and sadness! I couldn't believe it. It was the heaviest I'd ever been. I didn't know what to do with myself. I found my body and, sometimes, even my face disgusting.

Fast forward ten years later, and I have been through the ringer trying to lose those 30 pounds... plus 50 more. It's been a struggle. I would lose some, but then gained more. This went on and on over the years. As of today, I have lost the majority of it, but I'm not 120 pounds again, nor am I a size 4. I hope to be again, someday, but it's ok if I'm not.

I have had to learn to see myself with love, no matter what I look like on the outside. I have developed who I am on the inside so much more, that I believe I am far more beautiful now. Also, I can honestly look in the mirror and see the good qualities about myself without focusing on the imperfections. I have become this way because of the tools Allison has talked about in this book. It took me a long time to accept these teachings and to put them into practice. But once I took the time to try it, not only did my whole perspective of myself and others change, I also immediately started losing weight easily. If you have any self esteem issues, I would definitely advise you to start the exercises she outlines right away.

I am so thankful that I was able to learn about and practice the 3 day challenge. Once I started, it became an everyday thing. Years later, it is simply a habit and part of my every day routine. I am happier and healthier. I am more accepting of myself and others. I am more thankful for my many blessings. I accomplish more in my life. I am also more full of love. Because of this, I can help make the world a better place. I have a thriving holistic healing business, and I teach these tools to many people dealing with the same body image issues I have dealt with and overcome. Thank you Allison!

Annette Anderson shares encouragement online here: https://www.facebook.com/nettiesnaturalhealing.

References

Gregoire, Carolyn. "How the Brains of Happy, Successful People Are Wired." The Huffington Post, October 1, 2015. http://www.huffingtonpost.com/entry/brain-connectivity-happy-successful-people_us_560c1757e4b0768127002b93.

WestJet. "Josh – Opening Doors and Hearts." WestJet Above and Beyond Stories, December 22, 2014.

Kersey, Cynthia. "Unstoppable Foundation." *Gratitude Series by Tiffany Peterson*, November 2015. GratitudeSeries.com.

Reynolds, Susan. "Happy Brain, Happy Life." *Psychology Today*, August 2, 2011. https://www.psychologytoday.com/blog/prime-your-gray-cells/201108/happy-brain-happy-life.

Mayo Clinic Staff. "Chronic stress puts your health at risk." Mayo Clinic, last modified July 11, 2013. http://www.mayoclinic.org/healthy-lifestyle/stress-management/in-depth/stress/art-20046037.

Babbel, Susanne. "The Connections Between Emotional Stress, Trauma and Physical Pain." Psychology Today, April 8, 2010. https://www.psychologytoday.com/blog/somatic-psychology/201004/the-connections-between-emotional-stress-trauma-and-physical-pain.

Whitaker, Morgan. "Back in the day: What critics said about King's speech in 1963." MSNBC, August 28, 2013.

http://www.msnbc.com/msnbc/back-the-day-what-critics-said-about-king.

Acknowledgments

I am so thankful for all the people that God has placed in my path to help me grow and learn throughout my life. I am grateful for my parents who taught me unconditional love and patience. I have had many dear friends over the years who have shown me great loyalty. My children have helped me to learn about true sacrifice and extreme joy. My husband has supported me without question in my journey.

I have been inspired on so many levels by my wonderful clients. They constantly remind me that no matter where we are in this life, there is always hope if we are willing to try. Each individual I have worked with has increased my understanding of God's love for His children.

I value my relationship with my Father in Heaven. My prayer is to be an instrument in His hands in serving and helping His children. I am so thankful for the ways He has provided for me, and fulfilled my prayers and desires. It is not always easy, but He has given me strength and support.

I feel extreme gratitude towards the mentors and coaches who have helped me to grow and become the person I am today. In chronological order they are J.R. Smith, Amber Peterson, Margie Squires, Kirk Duncan, Linda Curtis, Tammy Ward, David Fagan, and Amy Walker.

All of the people I have mentioned have helped to shape and impact my life in so many ways. Each of them, in a way, has been a soul mate, a person who has been placed in my path to help me along my journey in life. Without them, I would not be who I am today. Thank you.

About the Author

Allison H. Larsen is a highly sought after speaker, author and leading Intuition Expert. Her diverse background as a Reiki Master, Certified Personal Trainer, Yoga Instructor and Reflexologist give her a unique skill set to serve the world every day.

Allison has helped thousands of clients all over the world find greater success in their lives by teaching them to tap into their Soul Intuition through classes, mentoring, and speaking. She has been featured on many television shows and magazines as a guest expert. She enjoys traveling and spending time with her four beautiful children and handsome husband.

If you would like to connect with Allison for treatment, training, or speaking engagements, visit soulintuition.com.

www.ingramcontent.com/pod-product-compliance
Lightning Source LLC
LaVergne TN
LVHW051832080426
835512LV00018B/2827